Learning to
Pray

Carolyn Shealy Self
& William L. Self

A Handbook for Personal
and Group Study

Copyright © 1999
Ministerial Association
General Conference of Seventh-day Adventists

Originally published by Word, Incorporated, Waco, Texas, in 1978. All copy has been reset and repaginated.

PRINTED IN U.S.A.
Pacific Press Publishing Association
Nampa, ID 83687

ISBN 1-57847-055-2

Dedication

To our parents, who first taught us to pray:
Elsie and Clarence Shealy
Della and Robert Taylor

Acknowledgments

We want to express appreciation to the people of the Wieuca Road Baptist Church who participated in the pilot prayer groups. They have agonized with us and encouraged us through the "labor and delivery room" stages of this book. Without Dorothy Reeves, our secretary and dear friend, we could never get anything to press.

Contents

Preface

Jogging is boring. It may be good for the body, but it turns the mind to putty. A couple of years ago I began participating in this boredom. Actually, what I do cannot be called a "jog"—I shuffle. This shuffling is done along with a fitness program in which different exercises are performed, and the progress is noted faithfully on a chart (heart rate per minute, repetitions per pound, etc.) measuring the change in the physical dimensions of my life. One day during this self-imposed torture—about the fourth lap—it occurred to me: Why not measure the spiritual dimensions of my life as well as the physical? There must be some way to do the same thing for the other vital dimensions in one's life.

Of course, it doesn't seem very spiritual to *measure* the religious life. Things religious and spiritual, some shallow-minded, self-appointed religious leaders proclaim, should not be measured. To discipline and measure the religious life, they declare in their morning Bible studies, is not spiritual because it is inhibitive and keeps the spirit from freely acting in our lives.

This heresy has been pushed on the current generation of religious illiterates until they have become as stable as the leaves in the fall wind. What is needed is some discipline in the religious life, I reasoned. We need to build muscle, not have another "great experience." Two laps later everything fell into place. Why not build a discipline around the six petitions of the Lord's Prayer? Jesus intended this prayer as a lesson in praying in answer to the request, "Lord, teach us to pray," not as a liturgical exercise. I went off to a mountain retreat and spent two days developing the study pattern. When I got it into place, I decided to walk over an unused golf course with notebook in hand and to pray in the pattern of prayer that had been worked out around the Lord's Prayer. I resolved, on a nine-hole golf course, to pray one petition per hole and take the last three holes for summation. I thought that if I spent this much time walking and praying, surely by the time I finished I would be seeing blazing lights in the sky or babbling in an unknown tongue somewhere off in the trees. But I found it did not occur this way. Actually, after I had spent three hours walking the golf course praying and correcting the pattern for prayer that was being developed, I found that I came away heavily burdened because I realized how inadequate my past prayer life had been and how heavy the experiences of life were becoming. I spent some time sitting by a creek thinking it through.

Carolyn and I began working on this project together at this point. We each had a prayer notebook, and also each enjoyed our own copy of John Baillie's *A Diary of Private Prayer* and Harry Emerson Fosdick's *The Meaning of Prayer.* We like to have our own copies to mark meaningful passages. So we worked separately yet together during the next six months of trial-error and development. That period of time was exciting and adventurous for us. It was also a time of deep soul-searching for we were walking through some hard times. This prayer experience became so meaningful to us that we began to search for a way to share this with others.

At our fall Deacons' Retreat I casually mentioned that I wanted to try a pilot project with this spiritual discipline and requested that any who were interested in participating meet me before the evening worship service. Twenty people came, and we began developing our own prayer life around this pattern for prayer that Jesus had given. This group stretched into eight weeks, and when I asked them to dissolve so I could start with another group, they wouldn't quit. So my wife was drafted to continue the group for another five weeks.

I went through four groups this way. Each time I was able to refine the program a little more. Carolyn has led eight prayer groups, and we have observed that each group is different, yet alike. As I look back over my shoulder now, some very happy and exciting things have occurred.

First of all, I think we have put prayer in its theological

perspective. It's not a matter of getting prayers answered, but it's having the pray-er answered—developing a relationship with God in the midst of whatever life may bring. There was a real estate executive who was able to survive losing a multi-million-dollar company because he walked through this prayer pattern with a significant group. There were two young men, each of whom had lost his father by death, who worked through their grief in the group, particularly when we studied "Our Father." Another young man told me, as he came into the group, that he could not communicate with God. At the conclusion of the study, he said that the petition on "Our Father" helped him to understand that because he was not able to communicate with his earthly father, he had had difficulty developing a relationship with his heavenly Father. A Ph.D. in a local institution became terribly upset with the group experience and tried three times to quit. Each time the other members convinced him to remain, until finally, he left the church. Six months later he came to me and apologized and, with tears in his eyes, said that it was the prayer-workshop experience that had given him new life and a new spiritual dimension. But he had fought it all the way.

One older lady who looked very unhappy and tense attacked the study with a vengeance. Before the end of the workshop we commented that she looked different. She really did. Gone were the worried, tense lines; she looked years younger, but best of all she looked relaxed and happy and at peace inside.

When our first group of deacons and wives assembled, there was one widow of a former deacon. She was still hurting not only from the accidental death of her husband, but more recently the sudden death of her college son. Her testimony is one you will read about in the section "I Can't Get Through to God." We have watched reverently as she has worked through depression, anger, disappointment, and doubt. She has taught us all a great deal about living one day at a time and grappling with the real issues of the hard facts of life. Some days she soars, but many days she's doggedly hanging in there coping. This prayer discipline has been her sanity, she says. She is a truly beautiful person with the depth and understanding of life that is a rarity.

As yet we have not seen blazing lights, no one has had a mystical experience, and we are a bit shy on flashes of inspiration; but we have seen a lot of people find wholeness. We have found a lot of personal strength and, frankly, I've been able to carry some of the heaviest burdens that I've ever had, both personally and in the parish, because I've been a student in the school of prayer.

I think it is easier to jog than it is to pray, for jogging makes the muscles ache, but praying around the pattern of the Lord's Prayer can become a life-changing experience.

Introduction

*P*rayer is a power, a resource, and a privilege that is sadly neglected. Many of us are like Voltaire who was generally regarded as an infidel. When a religious procession carrying a crucifix passed him, he tipped his hat. A friend questioned him about his relationship with God and he replied: "We salute, but we do not speak." We acknowledge God, believe in the church, and hope he hears our cries in times of personal crisis, but we have no personal fellowship (friendship) with God as our father.

The results of relationships with family and friends are cumulative with the years. When we lose contact with a friend or family member, we never really forget them, but it takes many long letters, phone calls, or visits to catch up, renew, and revitalize the relationship. So it is with God our Father. Jude wisely exhorts us to "Keep yourselves in the love of God" (v. 21).

We have the privilege of learning to pray just as the disciples asked Jesus to teach them. They were so impressed by his power in prayer that this is the one thing they asked to be taught.

The disciples, being devout Jews, had a great heritage of prayer. They knew well the teachings of the religious leaders on prayer. They knew the formalized times to pray set by the teachers. They traced the morning prayer back to Abraham (Gen. 19:27); the noontime prayer was ascribed to Isaac (Gen. 24:63); and the evening prayer time was traced to Jacob (Gen. 28:11).

The Jews were a praying people who had absolute confidence that God yearned for their prayers. "The Lord is near to all who call upon him, to all who call upon him in truth" (Ps. 145:18). "When he calls to me, I will answer him; I will be with him in trouble, I will rescue him and honor him" (Ps.

91:15).

All through the Old Testament runs the idea that in praying man must be aware of the holiness and the glory of God; man must have the desire to obey and please God and to bring love, gratitude, and penitence. Moses gave a marvelous example of perseverance and persistence in prayer.

"But the Lord was wroth with me for your sakes, and would not hear me: and the Lord said unto me, Let it suffice thee; speak no more unto me of this matter" (Deut. 3:26, KJV).

"And I fell down before the Lord, as at the first, forty days and forty nights: I did neither eat bread, nor drink water, because of all your sins which ye sinned, in doing wickedly in the sight of the Lord, to provoke him to anger. For I was afraid of the anger and hot displeasure, wherewith the Lord was wroth against you to destroy you. But the Lord hearkened unto me at that time also" (Deut. 9:18-19, KJV).

"Thus I fell down before the Lord forty days and forty nights, as I fell down at the first; because the Lord had said he would destroy you. I prayed therefore unto the Lord, and said, O Lord God, destroy not thy people and thine inheritance, which thou hast redeemed through thy greatness, which thou hast brought forth out of Egypt with a mighty hand" (Deut. 9:25-26, KJV).

Even with all their heritage and knowledge of prayer, the disciples desired to be taught by Jesus. They felt, even as we do, inadequate to express themselves before God. They sensed the close intimacy of Jesus and the Father, and they yearned for this communication also. So often we are hesitant about praying. We don't know how or what to say, and so we fall back into a prayer memorized in childhood or get involved with a lot of religious words to cover our inarticulateness. We need to put our thoughts and feelings into words.

Many times our praying becomes only a "squeaky wheel" prayer. Whatever is bothering us most at the time gets all of our attention. We forget that there are other areas of life; we fail to pray for others or to express gratitude; we never bring our fellow sufferers before the Father. We focus only on the area of most severe pain. When this problem is resolved or removed, we forget to pray until we are hurting again. In between we "say our prayers" or beg God for something that we desire.

Prayer should be a habitual attitude, not a spasmodic demanding for God's goodness. Prayer should be communion with God, the feeling that God is always with us. We do not have to wait for a special place or to be in a certain posture. We shouldn't need to wait till all is quiet to get ready to pray because God is available as our constant companion. We don't always have to be talking to him because communion is not one-sided. If our lives are focused in an attitude of prayer, we can have the comforting "feeling" of his presence and he will communicate with us.

Jesus taught his disciples by example. His life was constant communication with the Father. The disciples saw the power Jesus received from prayer. They saw his face transfigured while he was praying. They heard their names called by Jesus in prayer. These men wanted to pray like Jesus. It is good for us to examine briefly the prayer habits of Jesus recorded by Matthew, Mark, Luke, and John. These writers (especially Luke) emphasized the human Jesus—how he prayed when he was here on earth surrounded by our same circumstances and temptations. Take the time to read these in your own Bible:

Luke 3:21, 22: While he was waiting in prayer, he received the Holy Spirit.

Mark 1:35: Jesus prayed for renewed energy and strength instead of sleeping an extra hour.

Luke 5:16: A better translation would read: "He was retiring to the deserts and praying." This means not a single act but a continuous habit. He was busy and pressured as we are, and he knew he had to have inner resources. He put prayer first and work second. What do you do?

Luke 6:12: Jesus was tired of the haranguing of the

scribes and Pharisees and felt the heavy burden of selecting the men who would be left to carry on his work. He found rest, fellowship, and a calming, wise counsel in communion with the Father.

Matthew 14:22; Mark 6:46: After an extremely tiring day beginning with the grief over the beheading of his cousin, John the Baptist, and ending with feeding the multitudes, Jesus was bone weary. Again he found rest in prayer.

Luke 9:18: Perhaps he was trying to teach his disciples to love to commune with God, also. He was pulling them closer. He probably desired human fellowship in prayer.

Luke 9:29: Jesus' face was radiant while praying. Our very countenance can change from hard and ugly to kind and gentle through prayer.

Luke 10:21: Jesus spoke to the Father with a joyous overflowing heart. Do we ever share the gladness of our lives with the Father?

Luke 11:1: The first step in learning to pray is to pray, "Lord, teach me to pray." How pleased Jesus must have been!

John 11:41: This demonstrates the certainty of his faith. This kind of faith comes only with close continuous contact with the Father.

John 12:27: Jesus forgets the crowds in his anguish. We see intense conflict and then complete surrender. And a quick answer from heaven which only the trained ear of Jesus could understand. Can you hear and understand the Father?

Luke 22:31, 32: Jesus had been praying for Peter by name. He is praying for each of us by name!

John 17: Here Jesus considers his work on earth finished and already he is praying the intercessory prayer.

Matthew 26:36-46; Mark 14:33-42: Jesus was in terrible agony praying, "Abba, Father if it be possible." What excruciating dread and horror Jesus must have felt as his sinless soul would be cut off from the Father for us. The mental, emotional, and spiritual agony was more than Jesus could bear. S. D. Gordon in his book *Quiet Talks on*

Prayer says that Jesus literally died of a broken heart. *Thy will be done.*

　　　Luke 23:34: He is thinking of others even in this agony.

　　　Mark 15:34: Jesus was separated from the Father by our sins.

　　　Luke 23:46: His last breath was a prayer.

It should be obvious after studying the prayers of Jesus that prayer is intensely personal. There are as many ways of praying as there are different individuals. We acknowledge no particular form but encourage the development of your own style. There is no one examination or test for all, but you must develop respect for your own natural prayer life. The only way anyone can communicate with God is through his own heart. We must clear the channels for God. We desire more than "back waters" of his Spirit.

Before we begin our detailed study of the Lord's Prayer, we should talk about praying "in Jesus' name." There is no other way to pray. We read in John 14:13, 14: "Whatever you ask in my name, I will do it." Acts 4:12 says: "There is salvation in no one else, for there is no other name under heaven given among men by which we must be saved." Matthew 18:20 promises: "For where two or three are gathered in my name, there am I in the midst of them." So our prayers are to God, our Father, in the name of Jesus.

Jesus gave the disciples a pattern—simple but very comprehensive. This was not just a liturgical form of words to be repeated but an outline for each individual to use in his own way.

The Lord's Prayer is the prayer that Jesus taught his disciples to pray. It is found in both Matthew and Luke and in both places it is in the context of the disciples. Matthew (6:9-13) places it just after the Sermon on the Mount, and Luke says that Jesus gave this prayer in answer to the request of one of his disciples (Luke 11:1-4). It cannot be meaningful to one who is not committed to Jesus Christ—it would be just a lot of words. Only a person who understands what he is saying and who is a disciple can sincerely pray this prayer. It could rightfully be called the Disciples' Prayer.

We will use Matthew 6:9-13 (King James Version) for our pattern. You will note that the later translations do not include "For thine is the kingdom, and the power, and the glory, for ever." This was not part of the original prayer according to the earliest and best manuscripts. However, it was added later as a response of praise by the congregation. This form of praise and worship dates back to David (1 Chron. 29:11) and is of great value in reminding us that God is all-powerful and that all the kingdoms of the world are his.

> After this manner therefore pray ye: Our Father which art in heaven, Hallowed be thy name.
> Thy kingdom come. Thy will be done in earth, as it is in heaven.
> Give us this day our daily bread.
> And forgive us our debts, as we forgive our debtors.
> And lead us not into temptation, but deliver us from evil: For thine is the kingdom, and the power, and the glory, for ever. Amen. (Matt. 6:9-13, KJV)

The petitions of the Lord's Prayer put things in proper perspective for us. The first three petitions put God in the center of the picture. They give God his proper place; they are for hallowing God's name, the coming of his kingdom, and doing his will. They make us stop and put God, not ourselves, in first place. Only then can we turn to our needs and desires. When God is given his proper place, all other things fall into their proper places.

The second part of the prayer deals with the three essential needs of mankind and lays them before the Father. These three petitions request help for our present needs—the physical maintenance of life, forgiveness for our past sins, and relief from fear and anxiety about the future. God must be in the center and then we bring to him our past, present and future. In these petitions we commit all of our lives to God.

I

Questions About Prayer

1

How Can We Pray?

All of us have heard people of great spiritual renown address their prayers in many ways from the lofty, pious, excessive effusiveness to the really improper "Dear Jesus." I say improper because it is quite clear in the words of Jesus that we are to address God as Father and make our prayers in Jesus' name (*through* him, not *to* him). We may want to express our awe and wonder of his holiness and greatness in such a manner as: "Oh, most Holy One; God of the Universe; Dear Heavenly Father." Note that the family term *Father* is used here. Our assurance that God the Father hears our prayers is in the words of Jesus himself in Matthew 18:19, 20. There is always one more present when praying is going on because Jesus is there. Even if we feel that we are too weak and sinful for the Father to hear us (and we shouldn't), we can rest assured that Jesus is there taking our prayer to the Father.

2

What About Prayer Promises?

When Jesus spoke in Mark 11:22-24 of having faith to move a mountain, he was saying: "Think of the most difficult situation you can imagine, pray about it, believing that God will answer and he will hear you." Don't stop here. Go on to John 14:13, 14 and read the words of Jesus: "*Ask anything* in my name." And now John 15:7 has a strong word: "If ye *abide* in me." *Abide* is the key word to all of our praying. This doesn't mean come to pay a courtesy call; it doesn't mean returning home for a summer vacation time or the Christmas holidays; it doesn't mean setting up temporary quarters or pulling a camper or travel trailer along. *Abide in me* means to move in lock, stock and barrel. It means commitment, moving in to stay forever. And this makes the difference. When we abide in him and his words abide in us, we can ask anything, and it shall be done. We often feel the need to hedge a little on this promise and worry about our faith when we come to these promises. We need not hedge at all. It is taken care of when we relax and begin to settle in the relationship. Things look different after you've unpacked the barrels and hung the drapes and placed the furniture. "Abide in me," he says, and then in this settled, comfortable relationship you can ask for anything.

John 16:23 and 24 verify the fact that God places no limit on who can ask or the kind of thing we can ask for. The only limits placed on prayer are implicit in these Scriptures. First, the prayer must be made *through* Jesus; second, the person must be totally committed to the Father in complete faith.

Something else we should remember about these prayer promises is that they were not made to the multitudes. These were spoken to the chosen disciples as Jesus tried to pull them aside more and more frequently to teach these men. These precious words are for the truly committed. This is where the difference comes. It is a matter of how much we allow the Father to have of us. They are not meant for anybody who just flies in and out of relationships, never staying to weep with the sorrowful, bind the wounds of the bleeding, or provide food or drink for the poor. Only those who have the courage and determination to walk through the Garden of Gethsemane, stand on that hill called Golgotha, and spill your very soul, your life, for the burdens of humanity, come through it all to the Resurrection Sunday hand in hand with the Father's son, Jesus; only those who have done that can know the deep meanings of the prayer promises.

3

"I Can't Get Through to God"

Before going any further in our study, we need to think realistically about why we sometimes feel unable to "get through" to God in our praying. Some of the problems will be discussed in greater detail under the appropriate steps, but we need to acknowledge now some of the difficulties we encounter.

Several people in our prayer groups have had difficulty getting past "Our Father." One of these men had to acknowledge and work through a very unhappy relationship with his earthly father. Many times grief over the death of one's father will have to be resolved before being able to really pray "Our Father."

Feelings of grief, unworthiness, anger caused by abandonment or ridicule from an earthly father, lingering rebellion toward parents or feeling unforgiven are just a few of the many obstacles we can encounter when we begin in earnest to pray as Jesus taught us.

How many times have you heard someone who is swallowed up in grief say, "If God is my Father, how can he allow these awful things to happen to me? Why does my child have leukemia? Why does my friend have multiple sclerosis? Why did God allow my neighbor's child to be hit by an automobile and killed? Why? Why? If God is my Father and if he really cares about his children, how can he allow these terrible things to happen?" Don't worry. It is all right to speak this way. The only way to have things settled is to put them openly and frankly before the Father. He does not reject us when we tell him our doubts . . . even when they include doubting his very existence. If we become closed and turn away from God there can be no communication.

When something terrible happens to us, we as Christians sometimes say, "God has done this to me." "God has taken away my husband." "God has sent this disease on me" and so on. This idea is definitely unbiblical. When sin caused the rift between God and man, sickness and heartache and death entered the perfect world. Each person has his own personal Garden of Eden experience when he is faced with his own selfish desires or the more difficult unselfish way of God. We turn to the glamorous, appealing, but hostile power and then blame God when the obvious wounds and torments come. When mankind is separated from God by sin, we are left to our own miserable world we create. *Everyone* is drawn into the great chasm of disorder caused by individual separation from God. The world brings judgment on itself, and we are victims of the chaos and turmoil.

However, God has not turned his back on his children. He knows our plight. One of the younger members of a prayer workshop declared that the only way he would be able to bear a personal tragedy would be to believe that it was God's will for his life. Blind acceptance, no questions asked, would be the only acceptable terms for him. Several others voiced this same opinion. That kind of acceptance sounds so noble and holy and Christlike. But as he expressed this view I was seething inside because Bill and I have walked through sheer hell a number of times in the past four years, and I cannot blindly accept the pain and anguish from God. I am speaking for myself, but as Bill and I went through this together, we cried out, "Oh, God, *why?* Why must we go through the Garden of Gethsemane and walk the hill to Calvary?"

At that point in the discussion my co-leader of the workshop (a graduate of our first experiment) could contain herself no longer. Four years ago Elaine's husband died tragically as the result of a heart attack brought on by bee stings. One hour he was working in the yard and the next he was dead, leaving Elaine with a son and three daughters. It was a painful recovery process for the whole family, learning to cope without a husband and father. Of course, their lives went on—groceries were bought, meals prepared, all the everyday unglamorous things that have to be done were taken care of. Family and friends undergirded the family with support. About fifteen months later the son, nineteen years old and a well-adjusted college student, had been killed instantly by a fall from a dormitory window. This seemed almost more than a human should be expected to bear.

Now in the midst of this workshop, Elaine turned to the young man who would tell her that this was God's plan. For the first time since these tragedies she talked about the way she felt and how she was still working with God through the pain and hurt. Something in her voice and her intenseness claimed the attention and the respect of everyone there. All of us were dabbing at our eyes to dry the tears. This is almost verbatim and you can sense that it is out of the overflow of a heart that is full. She said: "I cannot accept that God deliberately took my husband and my son in order to prove to me that 'all things work together for good to them that love him' (Rom. 8:28). [People insist on quoting the King James Version: "all things work together for good." Actually the more accurate and acceptable translation is from the Revised Standard Version, which says, "We know that in everything God works for good with those who love him, who are called according to his purpose."] I cannot take that. Well-meaning people said to me as I stood by the graves, 'It is God's will; don't cry.' My pastor, Bill, said to me: 'Lanie, I don't understand either. But we're going to talk through this with you. God loves you and we love you. We're with you.' Bill and Carolyn put their arms around me and loved me, and that's all I could handle. Sweet sugar-coated phrases are no help when your very soul is ripped apart. Don't ever do that to anybody. Just give your love and support.

"I've been angry with God and he knows it. I think the key to this prayer worship is being honest with God. If you refuse to face up and acknowledge your true feelings, then it is your loss. Nothing is hidden from the Father, but we miss the opportunity of communication with him if we are less than honest. One thing I've argued with God about is why did he take my husband and son and leave me? They are the winners. I'm left to cope and deal with reality."

God knows the suffering through illnesses or accident; he knows the anxieties that stalk us day and night; he knows the dark hours of loneliness that death and separation bring. He knows and is waiting for us to lift our hearts and minds out of our grieving and anger and look up to him. He is waiting and ready to love us, comfort us, and then lead us through a time of learning his way for our lives. We learn to turn to God and seek to understand what he is teaching us and what is in store for us. This is why a personal, daily walk with our Father is so important. Disasters and heartbreak are not devastating when we know that God, our Father, walks with us every step of the way, loving us, caring for us, and teaching us. Everything will be all right as long as we answer his calling to us and tell him everything.

4

Why Prayer Fails

*H*ow often have you heard it said, "Well, I prayed and nothing changed"? It is probably safe to say that everyone at one time or another has felt this way—that God has turned his back on us. If we are truly honest and face up to the truth about ourselves, we can find the reason, the hindrance to the prayer plan. Prayer is God and man uniting purposes to accomplish results. Our asking and expecting joined with God's doing bring about results that otherwise would not come to pass.

Sin hinders prayer. This should come as no surprise to us, but we blame God entirely when our prayers fail to bring results. Prayer is pulling with God to shape the world. Prayer is useless and a waste of breath if we are holding something in our lives that is displeasing to God. Sin can be defined as anything that separates us from God. The second petition of the Lord's prayer, "Hallowed be thy name," suggests beyond any doubt that our lives are to be lived to honor our heavenly Father. This in itself clears the channels of our lives so that God's love can come in and fill our hearts and we can be in constant prayer touch with God. Read Isaiah 1:15, Isaiah 59:1-3, Psalm 66:18.

James 4:2, 3 says that we receive not because we ask amiss. That is to say that we are selfish in our prayers. "Change my son. He bears my name and I want to be able to be proud of him." The motive is wrong.

Prayer can be offered for completely personal things such as healing, money, physical strength. God loves us and wants us to enjoy our lives to the fullest, but the motive determines whether our prayers are proper or not. The purpose of our prayers should please him. There are many reasons for perplexity in praying. The Bible clearly talks about these problems, and we are well aware of many of our own personal difficulties. "Your iniquities have separated between you and your God, and your sins have hid his face from you" (Isa. 59:2, KJV). "Blessed are the pure in heart: for they shall see God" (Matt. 5:8, KJV). "Therefore if thou bring thy gift to the altar, and there rememberest that thy brother hath ought against thee; Leave there thy gift before the altar, and go thy way; first be reconciled to thy brother, and then come and offer thy gift" (Matt. 5:23, 24, KJV). Here are a few others to help you search your own soul: harboring a grudge, wish for another's harm, envy, carelessness in conduct, bad thoughts, cherished sins (great or small), and selfishness.

Moods also have a great influence on our prayer life. Life is not built on a level so that we can maintain a constant elevation of spirit. There are mountains and valleys, emotional ups and downs. These are natural. Moods are the clouds of our lives; they will pass. Jesus went from transfiguration to hour of bitterness: "And about the ninth hour Jesus cried with a loud voice, saying, Eli, Eli, la-ma sa-bach-tha-ni? That is to say, My God, my God, why hast thou forsaken me?" (Matt. 27:46, KJV). Paul urged Timothy, "Be instant in season, out of season." Pray whether you feel like it or not. Pray when you are depressed and when you are feeling good about yourself.

One important consideration is the individual temperament. Every person must be allowed to pray his own way. We are each different and unique—God likes us that way. The Bible mentions a vast variety of prayer attitudes: kneeling (Acts 20:36); standing (Jer. 18:20); sitting (2 Sam. 7:18); prostrate (Matt. 26:39); silently (1 Sam. 1:13); aloud (Ezek. 11:13); in the Temple (2 Kings 19:14); in bed (Ps. 63:6); in fields (Gen. 24:11, 12); hillside (Gen. 28:18-20); battlefield (1 Sam. 7:5); riverside (Act 16:13); seashore (Acts 21:5); privacy (Matt.

6:6); practical (Neh. 1:3, 5); poets (Ps.); melancholy Jeremiah (Jer. 14:19); and radiant-spirited Isaiah (Isa. 12:2). Prayer is not reserved for a special class of persons. Each individual should cultivate in himself a respect for his own natural type of prayer.

The presence of God can be experienced only within our own hearts. God blesses us through our own capacities to receive and appropriate.

> If we love one another, God abideth in us (1 John 4:12).
>
> We are a temple of the living God; even as God said, I will dwell in them (2 Cor. 6:16).
>
> If any man . . . open the door, I will come in to him, and will sup with him, and he with me (Rev. 3:20).
>
> The water that I shall give him shall become in him a well of water (John 4:14).
>
> I cry unto God . . . I commune with mine own heart (Ps. 77).

The *only* way any man can commune with God is through his own heart. No one can experience the presence of God until he accepts the fact that God is seeking for him. The fifteenth chapter of Luke cites three instances of this. Our search for God is simply surrender to his search for us. We consent to be found by him.

5

Bloody Knuckles Praying

Can I pray about a burden more than once? People sometimes feel guilty about "bothering" God or being a nuisance. I am answering this from personal experience. For over four years I have prayed for someone to have a changed life. Before we started this study my praying was spasmodically hysterical but continuously desperate. The use of the workbook helped my praying become more logical even though it was still just as fervent. I began to be able to see small but definite changes in that person and finally after four years there is a great deal of difference with still more changing to come.

I had to strip my prayer of pride and really desire this change for the glory of God, not for my glory. This eliminated some of the trappings that seemed important to me. Not only do I pray for the change in the person, but I also pray daily that my contact with him will be a help and not a hindrance. So while I have continuously prayed this prayer, many changes have been made in many areas. This kind of praying is not in the same category with "vain repetitions." It may be repetitious, but certainly it is not vain. This situation is of soul-shaking importance to me and because my Father cares about me, he will not turn away from me concerning this matter. I have learned to talk to the Father about it and then not worry about it, but that doesn't mean that I am not still concerned or that I don't care. Some problems are so complex and some wounds are so deep that we get "bloody knuckles" from knocking at God's door.

Perhaps the following is a poor example but you can get the idea: Parents are used to hearing the "wants" of children but rarely do we run out and buy an expensive toy or dress or whatever at the first mention. We see if the interest is genuine or if it is just a whim. We don't buy expensive camera equipment unless there is a long-lasting interest and some talent displayed. Perhaps our Father wants to know that we are serious enough to ask over and over again.

There is also the question of whether or not we should continue praying for people with whom we have lost contact. That is a personal matter, but I feel that I may be the only one carrying that person's name before the Father. I may not know the person's needs, but the Father certainly does. One of the members of a workshop told us this true story: She lived in London and her pastor walked from his home to the church every day. Along the way he had to pass through some rough sections of town, and as he passed one particular bar there was always the same man loitering outside, very drunk and very loudmouthed. The pastor was really angry at the wasted life and annoyed by the obnoxious taunts of the man. He started praying for the man every time he saw him. This went on for years. Finally, one day this man appeared in his study and said, "They say you have been praying for me every day and I want to know why you would bother to pray for a man like me." The pastor was able to witness to the man and lead him to Christ! What if he had given up hope and stopped praying?

I think that if we really think of God as our Father, we need never hesitate to talk to him about all the things that concern us. It may be like a friend who said to me: "I hated to do it, but this morning at my prayer time I said: 'Father, we've got to talk about Mary again today.'"

Don't feel guilty—the Father wants to hear whatever you have to say. Remember that being bored and disgusted are human traits.

6

What Happens to People Who Pray?

*H*ave you ever thought about what might happen to you if you really start praying and building a deep relationship to God the Father? Here are some examples from the Bible for you to consider: (1) Genesis 15:2-6, Abraham praying for heir; (2) Genesis 18:22-33, 19:29, Abraham interceding; (3) Genesis 32:24-32, Jacob wrestling with God; (4) 1 Samuel 1:10-18 and 26-28, Hannah praying for a child; (5) 1 Kings 3:6-14, Solomon prays for wisdom; (6) 1 Kings 17:20-24, Elijah praying for healing; (7) Daniel 2:12-19, Daniel asking his friends to pray for his understanding; (8) Daniel 6:13-22, Daniel in the lions' den; (9) Jonah 2:1-10, Jonah in the belly of the big fish; (10) Acts 12:5-7, Church praying for Peter; (11) Acts 28:8, Paul praying for healing power; (12) Luke 6:12, Jesus praying all night before big decision; (13) Luke 9:28-32, Jesus prayed and his countenance glowed; (14) Luke 22:39-46, Jesus agonizing in prayer; (15) Luke 23:34, 46, Jesus on the cross. These scriptures show that many times unusual things happen to people who pray. In fact they sometimes end up in strange and awful places (lions' den, the cross, etc.). Are you willing to take that risk? Meditation and self-hypnosis can bring serenity, but what about those times when you need strength just to endure? We want power, not serenity. Prayer is not just saying a few words and letting it be; it is mental and emotional and spiritual battle, hammering out our relationship with God, our

Father. Other religions promise inner peace, serenity and security. Christianity cannot promise that. True prayer may get you in the lions' den, or in prison for speaking out in righteous indignation on a moral issue; it may make you extremely unpopular with your peer group; you may smolder with unanswered questions from God. True prayer is no less than wrestling with God for your very life. Any other way is playing the ostrich and trying to ignore the great, plaguing issues and problems that hound us. Do you dare to pray?

I have a very close friend who not long ago found herself in an unbelievable situation. To her and her family it seemed that death would have been easier to face. This family along with loving, understanding friends had prayed for over five years for a prodigal son who, under the influence of friends and drugs, was sliding closer and closer to the brink of disaster. They prayed with bloody knuckles for a change in the boy's life. The years were marked by fear, hopelessness, violence, shame and despair. It looked as if God had lost his power to change this rebel's life. For people who have never known this anguish, please thank God to have been spared and be generous with your understanding and love. How often I have prayed with my friend and heard her plead with God to bring her son to his senses, to claim him again. She had long ago learned that she had to turn him over to the heavenly Father. The family had done all that was humanly possible to the point of bankruptcy both monetarily and emotionally.

Now here they were waiting to go into the courtroom to stand with this troubled son before the judge. As they waited, they watched people go in as free men and women and come out and walk down the hall handcuffed to an officer to go off to jail. As their turn came closer, they seemed to be braced and hardly breathing. The son, penitent at last, was pale and trembling. My friend kept mumbling over and over, "I can't believe this is happening to us. I can't believe it." I couldn't believe it, either. These were good people who had tried as best they could to be good examples and teach their children not only right from wrong, but the ways of the Lord.

Then they stood before the judge who had all the power in this matter. They spoke in loving support of their child. Gone were the friends to whom he had paid allegiance. All had deserted him and this rebellious son saw that only his family, a teacher, and one close friend surrounded him. As the judge pronounced sentence, one chapter closed and another began. As my friend has said so many times since those days of torment, "When I prayed for God to change my son, I had some other way in mind. I would never have believed that I was praying to end up in a court and a jail." God knows his children and only he can be wise enough and powerful enough to be with us in the lions' den and bring us and our loved ones through the experience with changed lives.

What happens to people who pray? As we talked about this one evening in a prayer group, a lovely young woman spoke up shyly and said, "I am the living result of my adopted mother's prayers." We encouraged her as she began to tell with great emotion this dramatic story (I have condensed it for our purposes here): Joan was born into a very poor family who already had nine children to care for. They lived in an abandoned railroad car, food was practically nonexistent, and neither parent had a job. The father said that they would have to sell the new baby.

Not too far away lived a couple who had never had any children. The husband worked as a miner and the wife, who was very obese and diabetic, made pies for the luncheon counter of a variety store. This woman had prayed for years for a baby and now with her increasing age and poor health it looked as if God had never heard her. Her husband heard a rumor about there being a baby for sale and told his wife about it. They found the place where the people lived and offered to take the baby, but the father said he had to sell her. Of course, this was against the law, and the couple said they could not buy the baby even though it nearly broke their hearts to leave the tiny, undernourished child who now had pneumonia. Well, days went by and the couple continued to pray about this baby and finally the mother of the baby called her and said, "Please come and get the baby. No one will pay money for her, and she is so sick she will die tonight if she isn't cared for." A lawyer friend got the proper papers to be signed, and the couple got the baby legally. Somehow in all the rumors the welfare department heard about the situation and, after the papers had legally been signed and filed, tried to make the baby a ward of the court. During all this the newspaper made headlines of the story and the caption under the picture was something like: "Father tries to sell baby." Joan looked around at us and said, "I later saw that picture and asked my adopted mother if that was a baby bird. She told me that it was a picture of me when she took me home with her. She didn't think I would live because of malnutrition and pneumonia. My natural father spent time in prison because of this situation. I never knew my natural parents. To me, my adopted parents are my real parents. They loved me and cared for me and my mother taught me to pray and read the Bible. I owe my very life to a woman who believed in prayer."

What happens to people who pray? Are you ready to find out for yourself?

II

The Lord's Prayer

7

Our Father

Our Father, which art in heaven (Matt. 6:9, KJV).

J esus Christ, God's son himself, teaches us this prayer. Only if we accept Jesus as the Son of God can we pray "Our Father," because Jesus, in his life, death, and resurrection, is the guarantor that there is a Father. We must come to God as Father through our relationship to Jesus. We can address God the same way Jesus did through the Holy Spirit (Mark 14:36, Rom. 8:15, Gal. 4:6). We would all be orphans if Jesus had not opened the gates of heaven to us. Jesus came to be the Father's messenger, to teach us, and to make us fit for heaven. We are not orphans. God is "Our Father" who calls us by name.

If you ever feel lonely, alone, desolate, or orphaned, read these scriptures to be reassured that God is Father. They settle our *relationship* to God. Read them in your Bible, thinking about your relationship to *Our Father*.

Jesus prayed for us saying, "Thou hast loved them even as thou hast loved me" (John 17:20-23).

Your father knows what you need before you ask (Matt. 6:5-14).

Our Father knows our needs and will provide. Do not worry (Matt. 6:25-33).

Even the hairs of your head are numbered (Matt. 10:29-31).

Stresses God as Father giving good gifts (Matt. 7:7-11).

We are the heirs of God; fellow-heirs with Christ. This

is a rich heritage we can claim (Rom. 8:14-17).

God knows the names of his children (Ex. 33:17; Isa. 45:3).

We can address God the same way Jesus did—through the Holy Spirit. Abba is the intimate Arabic term for Father used even today, like Dad or Papa (Mark 14:36; Rom. 8:15; Gal. 4:6).

God's love is undeserved. He reaches out to the son who rebels and breaks his heart. He is waiting with open arms when the rebel comes home at last because there is no other place to go (Luke 15:11-32).

Let these verses come alive and be meaningful to you.

The use of the term *Abba* (Daddy, Papa) settles our relationship to God. He is our Father; we become his sons or daughters through the invitation of Jesus to pray *Our* Father; that includes us in his family—Jesus' brothers or sisters. Jesus didn't say, "Pray this way: 'Dear God, Father of Jesus.'" He gave us access to God by telling us to pray this way: "Our Father." This relationship assures us that God loves us no matter what we do; we do not deserve such love. The Father does not treat us as if we were lumps of clay to be thrown away, but as his children whom he loves in a special way. Jesus took the burden of our sin on himself so that we can go to Our Father in his name. Only as disciples can we pray to Our Father in Jesus' name. "Neither is there salvation in any other: for there is none other name under heaven given among men, whereby we must be saved" (Acts 4:12, KJV).

This term *Abba* also determines our relationship to our fellow human beings. God's family is all-inclusive—look around you at your family. The next time you are angered by someone or you doubt the worth of a person, stop and remember that in Our Father's eyes that person is valuable. He is God's child, too, and related to you! This is really the only true value of any person—that he is a child of God. We cannot pray "Our Father" and despise or hate any man; that would be a mockery. Actually, we cannot go further in our prayers until we can settle this matter in our hearts and minds. These words, *Our Father*, in their true meaning forbid us to do anything but love every man.

Day 1

> For you did not receive the spirit of slavery to fall back into fear, but you have received the spirit of sonship. When we cry, "Abba! Father!" (Rom. 8:15).
>
> And because you are sons, God has sent the Spirit of his Son into our hearts, crying, "Abba! Father!" So through God you are no longer a slave but a son, and if a son then an heir (Gal. 4:6, 7).

When we pray "Our Father" we immediately place ourselves in the family unit. In fact, this word *Father, Abba,* is the same word Jesus used to pray to God. *Abba* is used even today in Palestine by children addressing their father. It is the familiar, dear term children first learn to say—*Daddy.* Understanding this beautiful relationship can change the tone of life. My grandmother was the second of eleven children. I recently visited the five living children of that family and was impressed with their reminiscence of the individual love and care and provision made for each child by my great-grandparents.

Think of it. Our heavenly Father cares for each of us—me with my problems, you with your unhappiness. Our Father knows me by my name and you by your name. He knows how many hairs are on each of our heads. He knows when I am embarrassed and when you are overcome with fear.

It is time for us to appropriate our Father's heritage given to his children who claim it.

Our Father, how your heart must be grieved to see how we ignore the heritage you have for us as your children. Forgive me, Father, when I ignore your presence. I guess it must be the way I would feel if my son came to the dinner table and never acknowledged my presence. Let me be more sensitive and

*appreciative of the bounty and beauty you provide. In Jesus'
name. Amen.*

Day 2

Are not two sparrows sold for a penny? And not one of
them shall fall to the ground without your Father's will. But
even the hairs of your head are all numbered. Fear not,
therefore; you are of more value than many sparrows
(Matt. 19:29-31).

When our older son was about two or three years old, we
lived in south Florida. One night we were wakened by a
terrible thunderstorm and by the frightened cries of Lee. We
went to his room and found him standing at the end of his
crib sobbing louder with each flash of lightning. My husband
lowered the side of the crib, took Lee in his arms and held
him close. As he walked up and down the hall talking to him
softly and patting him gently, Lee's head soon nestled on his
father's shoulder, his rigid back relaxed, and he was sleeping
peacefully—in his father's arms.

When the storms of life leave us sobbing and quivering,
we can be *sure* that our heavenly Father responds to each
child. He is there waiting with open arms to protect and
comfort each child.

God not only created the vast universe but he is aware of
and cares about every individual thing. He cares about a
worthless sparrow. He knows *you* by name and longs to have
you come to him as child to parent.

*Oh, Father, the storms of life blow and there is destruction
all around. My whole life seems to be falling apart. How could
I go on living if I could not go home to you, Father? I am tired
and need to rest my head on your shoulder. Give me respite
and the grace to open my life to you so that I may claim the
heritage of being your heir. In Jesus' name. Amen.*

Day 3

A wise son makes a glad father, but a foolish son is a sorrow to his mother (Prov. 10:1).

If you then, who are evil, know how to give good gifts to your children, how much more will the heavenly Father give the Holy Spirit to those who ask him! (Luke 11:13).

Recently I was visiting a friend whose daughter is taking her last year of high school in a boarding school. The telephone rang, and I couldn't help hearing the tense, tired tone of her voice as she talked intently for a long time. When she returned to continue our visit, she looked weary and sad. All of her former enthusiasm was gone. Finally she said: "That was Sally. The minute I hear her voice I know it's trouble. When she calls, it is to complaint about her studies, her teachers, her friends, the food, the weather—whatever it is, she makes it my responsibility. If only she could share something good with me once in a while." I made a mental note to examine my prayer life. Am I any better than Sally? Don't forget how you as a parent enjoy being told about the good things that come to your children and about their happy times as well as their bitter defeats and secret sorrows.

How patient our heavenly Father is with our whining and complaining. When will we outgrow our adolescent haranguing?

Dear Father, help me outgrow my adolescent attitudes. I know that you care about me. Now let me begin to learn to appropriate the privilege of conversation with you. Let me know you and love you and cast out the fears that keep me from maturing. In Jesus' name. Amen.

Day 4

And he said, "There was a man who had two sons . . ." (Luke 15:11).

These words begin a story that is not unfamiliar to many families. The story includes rebellion, jealousy, heartbreak, repentance, return, acceptance and rejoicing. Do any of these adjectives describe what is going on in your family? This story, known as the Prodigal Son, is read quickly. Here in twenty-one verses we are able to see the beginning and the end.

Many of us are filled with rebellion or jealousy. But our heavenly Father knows the pain and heartache of wayward children. We must be aware that God will hearken to our needs and will sustain us. God is not isolated and detached. He is involved, and he cares with the constant love of a Father.

"A man had two sons"—God has two kinds of sons. He has sons who break his heart and sons who delight his heart. There are such wonderful things for the obedient sons; the disobedient son can never know these precious gifts until he returns to his Father's love.

Oh, Father, where could I turn, what would I do without your constant love? I would be desolate, desperate. This one who is being bruised and battered, Father, is your child also. Open his heart and mind, put your thoughts in him; let him glorify your name with his life.

Thank you, dear Father, that we are not too small or insignificant for you to know us individually.

Let the words of my mouth and the meditations of my heart be acceptable to thee, Father. In Jesus' name. Amen.

Day 5

> And he arose and came to his father. But while he was
> yet at a distance, his father saw him and had compassion,
> and ran and embraced him and kissed him (Luke 15:20).

The rebellious son went as far away from home as he could, and he must have been very disillusioned when his peers deserted him one by one. Why are we always amazed when this ancient fact of life is proven again and again? Who enjoys your success? Who remains through troubled times?

Whom do you turn to when you are desperate? Let's face it—
my human family and my church family are always standing
by ready to walk with me or even carry me through the tough
times. This love is undeserved. Our heavenly Father so
graciously has provided tangible, earthly help and comfort for
us in our families and in the church of our Lord Jesus Christ.
These are part of God's caring—of his loving touch. Where
else can I go for help and comfort and not be scorned or put
down? They represent the father running to greet the rebel,
embracing and kissing him.

*Our Father, each day this endearing term grows more
precious. It immediately makes me your child and places me
in a family of loving, caring individuals. Though I rebel and
lash out at you and those who love me, you (and they) will be
waiting, watching for me to come home. Oh, Lord, let me rest
in the security of your love now. I am ready to be a mature,
responsible member of the family. In Jesus' name. Amen.*

Day 6

But the father said to his servants, Bring quickly the
best robe, and put it on him; and put a ring on his hand,
and shoes on his feet; and bring the fatted calf and kill it,
and let us eat and make merry; for this my son was dead,
and is alive again; he was lost, and is found. And they
began to make merry (Luke 15:22-24).

A new baby soon learns the cry that keeps everyone
jumping to feed, change, rock, snuggle and love him. As he
progresses to the toddler stage, he still has the family fairly
well controlled. As parents we become anxious for each baby
to walk and talk. We desire the child to mature and grow
through each stage to become a creative, responsible adult.

Through the adolescent years we get fleeting glimpses of
the forming, struggling character that is being pressured on all
sides. What pleasant relief, however brief, to see evidence of
that strong will being focused properly.

It is such a pleasure when children grow into adults and there are times of quiet conversation, sharing of ideas. Who else in all the world could understand better the whys and wherefores of one's background except his parents?

Let's be finished with being in grade school, terrible teens, doubting swingers, etc. Let's come home to sit at our heavenly Father's feet.

Let's pour out our hearts—the joys, sorrows, successes, failures, ecstasies, and disappointments. We don't have to worry about how to say it—let it tumble out. The joy will be both for us and God. He desires communion with his children; his heart also longs for them to come home.

Dear Heavenly Father, may I never let the familiar become neglected. I may pray any time—let me not fail to take advantage of this opportunity and privilege. You made me. My heart is restless until it rests in thee. In Jesus' name. Amen.

Day 7

And he lifted up his eyes, and saw his brother Benjamin, his mother's son, and said, "Is this your youngest brother, of whom you spoke to me? God be gracious to you, my son." Then Joseph made haste; for his heart yearned for his brother, and he sought a place to weep. And he entered his chamber and wept there. Then he washed his face and came out; and controlling himself he said, "Let food be served" (Gen. 43:29-31).

When we utter the words *Our Father*, we settle not only our relationship to God but also our relationship to our fellowman. The word *our* placed before Father ends all snobbery, nationalism, racialism, hatred and exclusiveness. The only value that any person has is that he is a child of God. This privilege is denied to no one. Every human being can be sure that his heavenly Father will acknowledge him.

When have we been like Joseph and yearned for a "brother"? When have we wept for the soul of a "family" member?

One Saturday afternoon at a football game my mind wandered, and as I looked around the stadium full of people I thought about them as God's children, too. About that time a grossly overweight lady crawled over me leaving heel prints in my foot, the cigar-puffing man behind me yelled an obscenity, the man to my right got so excited he nearly beat me to death. I observed that some couples were well-dressed and charming, and others were tacky and ill-mannered. And I thought, "Our Father"? How can God stand us? There we were, thousands of people screaming and hollering, little puffs of smoke rising from all over the stadium like incense, and a bunch of guys dressed in pads and helmets fighting over a ball and sustaining serious injuries. I suddenly remembered Dr. William Barclay's statement: "The only possible basis for democracy is the conviction of the fatherhood of God." He goes on to say that if we pray, "Our Father," and hate or despise our fellowman, then the prayer is a mockery and we make ourselves liars.

Our Father, thank you for making it so clear that all men have the right and privilege to call you Father. I thank you that I can be sure that no matter where I am or what I do, your love will never let me go. I do not deserve it, but I desire it. Keep me in thy love through Jesus. Amen.

8

Hallowed Be Thy Name

Hallowed be thy name (Matt. 6:9, KJV).
But sanctify the Lord God in your hearts (1 Pet. 3:15).

We all live lives in which God's name is not honored. We place more importance in the name of the boss and in today's historymakers. We also give activity the place of honor in our lives. A display of good works and accomplishments makes us look really good. Life can get to be a merry-go-round of endless frantic activity to keep up the show. No wonder we become disillusioned and run out of steam in the middle of a "do-good" project. We get on this treadmill when our prayer is "Lord, let me be a good, devout person." This puts us in the center. The harder we try to have high ideals, to do good works, to be a good person, the more we feel a vacuum. We need to change our prayer from "Let me be honored" to "Thy name be honored." Then we understand the source of life. Our destiny and our lives will be in proper order when we understand that Jesus taught us to pray, "Dear Father, let your name be holy and honored, not mine."

Without a doubt Jesus meant that we should not take the Lord's name in vain. If we limit our understanding of this petition to profanity, we have missed the most important point. "Hallowed be thy name" means that we are praying to the glory of God—not to ourselves. Unless we see these words as repentance on our part, we should go no further. We must understand the serious implications this petition has for our lives. We slide by it quickly hoping that God will not notice the dark corners, the shadowy places, the ideas, prejudices, attitudes which we so stubbornly cling to and hold dear to our hearts. The famous German pagan philosopher Nietzsche is not the only person who has said: "Show me that you are redeemed, and then I will believe in your redeemer."

"O come let us adore Him" are the words we sing at Christmas time. This should be the theme of our prayers— coming before our Father with an adoring, open life. We obviously adore things and money and relegate the things of God to second place at best. For instance, what is your attitude concerning your church and worship? Is it important? Or can you easily and quickly rationalize your absence? When you worship, are you an observer or a participant? The church is the body of Christ, his bride. Worship is not a stadium event; it is fellowship with God, our Father, and with each other. We need this desperately. Commit your life to the Father, and participation and reverence must follow.

Paul condemned Christians who dishonored God's name when he said: "The name of God is blasphemed among the Gentiles because of you" (Rom. 2:24). Today we hear people say that there are too many hypocrites in the church. When people see a person who claims to be a Christian living an immoral and unlovely life, they blame it on Christianity as a whole, not on the individual Christian. It is a sad commentary on our Father's name when a person who calls himself a Christian knowingly takes part in a dishonest business transaction, or when a Christian tears down another person's character by slurring or slanderous words. Only when we hallow God's name by making our hearts his dwelling place will our lives truly honor him. When this happens, people will see the difference in our lives, even in our appearance. Then we can drop the masks we wear so effectively and let the one who lives in us shine through.

Every Christian is the incarnation of Christ to those with whom he comes in contact. This truth seems to be very difficult for some people to accept. However, whether we accept

it or not, it is still true based on Scripture. Remember the Old
Testament when God used men and women to speak to the
people? The list could go on forever and would include
Abraham, Moses, Jacob, Deborah, Hosea. Then in the New
Testament God comes to man in the human form of Jesus—
God and man together. When Jesus died on the cross for our
sins, was buried and rose from the grave on the third day, he
gave us the Holy Spirit to dwell in each individual heart. If
you have accepted Jesus as your Lord and Savior and asked
him to come into your heart, he is there dwelling in you! You
cannot deny it—God incarnate (in the flesh)!

Paul says, "I have been crucified with Christ; it is no
longer I who live, but Christ who lives in me; and the life I
now live in the flesh I live by faith in the Son of God, who
loved me and gave himself for me" (Gal. 2:20). "To them God
chose to make known how great among the Gentiles are the
riches of the glory of this mystery, which is Christ in you, the
hope of glory" (Col. 1:27).

Some people have expressed the view that it is too
presumptuous, too bold and arrogant, to acknowledge this
incarnation. Let me assure you that it is not arrogance that
people are afraid of. We are afraid of the awesome responsibility of being the only Jesus someone may know. One
cannot refuse to accept this responsibility and be a Christian.
Jesus himself thrust it upon us when he taught us (Acts 1:8)
that we are to be his witnesses. Commitment and responsibility are two things that are not very popular now. We have
no choice if Jesus is living within us. The old phrase, "you
never know who is watching you," is valid. Our facial expressions, words and reactions to situations are always under
scrutiny. We cannot escape. "Hallowed be Thy name" states
the inescapable obligation of reverence in every area of our
lives.

Day 1

Therefore God has highly exalted him and bestowed
on him the name which is above every name, that at the

name of Jesus every knee should bow, in heaven and on earth and under the earth, and every tongue confess that Jesus Christ is Lord, to the glory of God the Father (Phil. 2:9-11).

Our attention this week is on "Hallowed be Thy name," and yet in no way can we pray these words without continually deepening our understanding of "Our Father."

One of the few things that each individual must have is his certificate of birth. All through life we have to prove over and over again that we were born and that we have parents who gave us a name. This certificate is so valuable that not only do we keep the original copy in a lockbox but there is a recording of this information in a courthouse somewhere.

Now if we pray "Our Father," Jesus is giving us a new certificate of birth. He is saying, "my Father is also your Father and his name is precious and holy." Jesus' whole life was dedicated to exalting the name of the Father.

There is no way for us to say "Our Father" if we do not know to whom we speak. Any person can speak of a God or acknowledge that there is a supreme being, but that makes God only an idea in the mind. They lack a birth certificate. If God does not seem real to you, perhaps it is because your certificate of birth is buried in the cedar chest under all those cherished but never used memories—the wedding veil, college degree, hand-made baby dress, certificate of baptism, your child's first letter home from camp, and the moth-eaten picture of your great grandparents. It's time to dig out your spiritual birth certificate and begin to inherit the riches of our Father.

Dear Father in heaven, again we thank you for the heritage you have given us through Jesus. You have relieved us from the intricacies of intellectual problems concerning prayer. Thank you for making it so simple to say "Our Father" and rest assured that there are no puzzles to solve or riddles to answer. Let me never bury my certificate of birth beneath ques-

tions, problems or memories. Thank you for your son Jesus who makes our prayers known to thee. Amen.

Day 2

Read 2 Samuel 12:1-9. Nathan said to David, "You are the man" (v. 7a).

God is my Father; his children are my family, but *who am I?* What are the things, the ideas, the activities, the secrets which make up my life?

We should all be very careful before signing our names to any document—the fine print is important. Look inside yourself now and see if you'd like to sign your name to your life. Be honest now—is that super pious attitude flashing neon signals that shout "sham"? Does your "goodness" turn sour when you are alone with only your family? Are you angry when people around you just won't do what you think is best for them? Are you careful that word doesn't get around at the office that you are a Christian? Do you ever try to imagine what it would be like to live with *you?* What are your secret areas of nonsurrender? Write them down. Spend some time making a *who am I* document and honestly decide if you can sign your name to it.

Dear Father, help me to be honest and really try to see myself as others see me, but most of all as you see me. I do not want to dishonor your name by being glib or superficial in my relationships with people. I become the incarnation of you to those around me. Use my life to honor your name and keep it holy. In Jesus' name. Amen.

Day 3

And a ruler asked him, "Good Teacher, what shall I do to inherit eternal life? And Jesus said to him, "Why do you call me good? No one is good but God alone. You know the commandments: 'Do not commit adultery. Do not kill. Do not steal. Do not bear false witness. Honor your father

87256

and mother.'" And he said, "All these I have observed from my youth." And when Jesus heard it, he said to him, "One thing you still lack. Sell all that you have and distribute to the poor, and you will have treasure in heaven; and come, follow me" (Luke 18:18-23).

Having canceled the bond which stood against us with its legal demands; this he set aside, nailing it to the cross (Col. 2:14).

Sometimes we become so overwhelmed with our goodness, so busy with keeping our mask straight and keeping the secrets hidden that we become very impressed with ourselves and marvel at our goodness. The rich young ruler was a really good person. He felt pretty good about himself and probably thought he was well ahead in goodness compared to the motley crowd around Jesus. He had never been turned down by any person or group. He was the kind of young man that you'd like your daughter to marry. Surely Jesus would put his stamp of approval on his life. How sad for the rich young ruler that he turned sadly away with a bill of indictment. Jesus could have and would have canceled it for him on the spot.

Where are you? Would you be so bold to expect, even demand, that God sign his name to your life? Look at it again. What do you have to offer God? Scrape the filters off your eyes and recognize it for what it is—a bill of indictment.

Dear Father in heaven, all I have is a bill of indictment. How terrified I would be except I know by your word alone that Jesus Christ has canceled it. In Jesus' name I come to you. I become your child. Thank you, Father. I glory in this. Hallowed be thy name. Amen.

Day 4

"And they ask me, 'What is his name?' what shall I say to them?" God said to Moses, "I AM WHO I AM." And he said, "Say this to the people of Israel, 'I AM has sent me to you.'" God also said to Moses, "Say this to the people of

Israel, 'The Lord, the God of your fathers, the God of
Abraham, the God of Isaac, and the God of Jacob has sent
me to you': this is my name for ever, and thus I am to be
remembered throughout all generations" (Ex. 3:13b-15).

When Moses asked God what to say to the people when
they questioned his authority, God's answer was quick and to
the point and settled once and for all his unique, separate
nature. God made sure that no one would ever question his
authority, his character or personality.

God would lead the children of Israel out of bondage into
the promised land, but they had to believe him and act on
faith. When they became disenchanted and weary, cross and
irritable, and failed to honor God's name, they were
punished.

To doubt God's ability to deal in our lives and lead us into
the promised land of our tomorrow is to bring dishonor to
God's name. We make his name less than holy, a mockery,
when we refuse to take a stand that is unpopular but moral.
Whom is it important to please? Our heavenly Father or our
heathen neighbor? We have to know what our heavenly
Father is like. His love and care for us should enable us to
give to him the reverence his nature in our lives demands.

*Our Heavenly Father, let me put my trust in your name.
Let me continually work on a life that will reflect your
redeeming love. Hallowed be thy name through my life,
thoughts, words, actions—the whole tone of my life.*

*Thank you, Father, that we can know about you also from
studying the great people you have used in the past. Thank
you, Father, that in you we experience both your love and holiness through your son Jesus. Amen.*

Day 5

When I look at thy heavens, the work of thy fingers,
the moon and the stars which thou hast established; what
is man that thou art mindful of him, and the son of man

that thou dost care for him? O Lord, our Lord, how majestic
is thy name in all the earth! (Ps. 8:3-4, 9).

No doubt David was out tending his sheep, and as he
studied the night sky was overcome again with the order and
majesty of the universe. Throughout the ages men have tried
to verbalize the feeling of awe that is overwhelming when we
see the vastness of God's creation.

One of our teenage sons had a summer job in the north
Georgia mountains. He stayed alone most of the time and one
evening he called his grandmother long distance to describe
at length and in detail the gloriousness of the setting sun. It
is good for all of us to pull aside from the hustle and bustle
of everyday living and experience again the awareness of the
presence and holiness of God in his created world.

*I praise you and thank you, Father, for the beauty of the
earth: as I walk the mountainsides and the green valleys,
everywhere I look there is so much beauty I cannot absorb it
all; the grass is so green, the wind rustles the leaves, then
makes the branches sway; the brooks and streams gurgle and
converge into a waterfall cascading loud and hissing into the
lake below; the wind, water, and earth are so full—now I
know a little of the fullness of the earth.*

*Thank you, Father, for the glory of the skies: at dusk I see
the moon rising over the mountains casting new shadows and
hues over the trees and grass; night and day will surely
come—the same and yet always different.*

*Oh, Father, let me never take for granted any day or night
and may I never be the cause of an unhappy day or night for
anyone. To see, to smell, to feel the beauty of the earth and the
glory of the skies is truly the fullness of life and the love of our
heavenly Father. Hallowed be thy name! Amen.*

Day 6

Make a joyful noise to God, all the earth; sing the glory
of his name; give to him glorious praise! (Ps. 66:1, 2).

Let the nations be glad and sing for joy, for thou dost
judge the peoples with equity and guide the nations upon
the earth. God has blessed us; let all the ends of the earth
fear him! (Ps. 67:4, 7).

It is always the way of human beings to tell good news.
A good story or joke is no fun unless you can tell it to somebody. Jesus commanded his disciples to go into all the world
preaching, teaching and healing in his name. To know God's
name we must see to it that all nations have reason to sing
for joy. It is our obligation to spread the good news of Jesus
Christ throughout the world, but begin at home. Daily living
under the pressures of keeping it all together can make us
less than attractive to our family and community. Who has not
been guilty of acting out when confronted with a balky child,
overflowing washing machine and ringing telephone? In the
office when the secretaries are snippy, the boss is unreason-
able and you suspect that things are not above board, do you
retreat within yourself and add more fuel to the ulcer you're
working on? It's hard to live so that we honor our Father's
name in tough circumstances.

*Our Father, it is easy for me to pray that all nations will
praise thee—as long as you don't send me with the message.
Help me today to live so that those whose lives touch mine will
know that Christ is in my heart. Let your name be glorified in
my life through Jesus. Amen.*

Day 7

But sanctify the Lord God in our hearts (1 Pet. 3:15,
KJV).

A good man out of the good treasure of his heart
bringeth forth that which is good; and an evil man out of
the evil treasure of his heart bringeth forth that which is
evil; for of the abundance of the heart his mouth speaketh
(Luke 6:45, KJV).

Whatever we hold dear in our hearts quickly becomes very obvious in even a chance conversation. Grandparents always have a gallery of pictures to illustrate the latest antics of their precious ones. Sometimes the businessman knows only how to put a deal together. Whatever is the most important thing in our lives comes out whether it is social, money, family, church. Actions and words express the intent of the heart. Listen to the conversation of your friends and to your own. Out of the overflow of the heart the mouth speaks. What you read, think and see comes out of the overflow.

We cannot minister to people in need if we have nothing to offer. We can share only what we have known and experienced personally.

Dear Father, let me remember that when I pray "Hallowed be thy name," I must make my heart your temple and dwelling place. Let me never forget that I have an inescapable obligation of reverence. Help me as I accept the challenge to Christian action and commitment. In Jesus' name. Amen.

9

Thy Kingdom Come

Thy kingdom come. Thy will be done in earth as it is in heaven (Matt. 6:10, KJV).

*D*o not even breathe this prayer if you desire to stay the same way you are today. We become complacent and enjoy the ebb and flow of life as long as there are no big storms to capsize our lives. These words "Thy kingdom come, Thy will be done," slip through our lips easily without much meaning when times are good. It is difficult to realize that this prayer is really a mystery which affects the deepest part of our beings.

Thy kingdom come. How can God's kingdom possibly come in the midst of the strife, anxiety, despair, and decay right here in my own life, my own home, city and state? How can God's kingdom come in the middle of war in the Near East, starving multitudes in India, gross dishonesty in government, incurable diseases that stalk unsuspecting victims, and disasters that mutilate and kill innocent children? God comes to us in good times and bad times. Sometimes the terrifying, heartbreaking times are the good times for God's kingdom to come. Thy kingdom come.

The kingdom of God is mentioned forty-nine times in Matthew, sixteen times in Mark, and thirty-eight times in Luke.

Jesus came preaching the kingdom of God. This was his central message (Mark 1:14; Matt. 4:17; Luke 4:43).

The kingdom of God is personal and is worth any effort. We can accept or reject it (Matt. 22:1-14; Luke 14:16-24; Mark 12:28-34; Luke 9:61, 62; Matt. 13:24-30, 47); and we must do it individually (Luke 17:21; Matt. 13:31, 32).

The kingdom of God is worth any effort (Matt. 6:33; Luke 16:16; Matt. 11:12), any price (Matt. 13:44-46; Matt. 10:37; Luke 14:26), any sacrifice (Matt. 5:30; Luke 18:29; Mark 10:28-30; Matt. 19:27-30).

In order to enter the kingdom we must: recognize our own total destitution and put ourselves in God's hands; be willing to be persecuted for righteousness sake (Matt. 5:10); love God more than *anything* (comfort, security, etc.); have a childlike (not childish) spirit (Matt. 18:2, 3; Mark 10:14, 15; Matt. 19:14; Luke 18:16, 17). Some barriers to the kingdom are: hypocrisy or lip service (Matt. 7:21); an unforgiving spirit or holding on to a grudge (Matt. 18:23-35); and riches that fix attention on this world and possibly make one think he can buy his way in or out of any situation including the kingdom (Matt. 19:23, 24; Mark 10:23-27; Luke 18:24, 25).

The kingdom of God is the reign of God in individual lives. It is the personal obedience to the will of God in my life and in your life. The kingdom of God begins within *me* and within *you*. It cannot be stopped. It *will* come. Man can delay its coming but not stop it (Matt. 4:23; Matt. 10:1, 7, 8; Matt. 11:1-6; Mark 6:7; Luke 7:19-23; Luke 9:11; Matt. 12:28; Mark 4:26-29). The kingdom is universal with no national favoritism or racial distinctions (Matt. 24:14; Matt. 8:11; Luke 13:29).

The kingdom of God stretches the imagination. In our personal lives the kingdom of God is already within us. As individual kingdoms we come together as a body of kingdoms—the church. Because the church is made up of earthbound human beings we have to pray "Thy kingdom come" daily. We can never rest and say, "The kingdom has come and that is all." We say the kingdom has come (in Jesus and in my heart) and is here now and will continue to come in my heart and in the lives of men. It is past, present, and future. We

cannot be dreamers or theorists but always desiring the flow-
ering of the seed planted and prayed for today.

> Being asked by the Pharisees when the kingdom of
> God was coming, he answered them, "The kingdom of
> God is not coming with signs to be observed, nor will they
> say, 'Lo, here it is!' or 'There!' for behold the kingdom of
> God is in the midst of you" (Luke 17:20, 21).

The kingdom of God first comes in the heart and soul of
a person. It begins deep within, and then as it grows and
flourishes, it moves outward. One cannot see it happen; it is
not heralded with trumpets nor can you read about it in the
newspaper. When it is within your heart and soul, it will
permeate every area of your life. You cannot separate your
social, political, professional, or religious life from the
kingdom of God within. You cannot actually see grass grow,
but you know that it does grow because it has to be cut. You
cannot watch a bud burst into full bloom (with the naked
eye), but one day it is a bud and the next it is full blown.
Have you observed people who are searching, never at
peace, running from one church to another and from one
group to another? They are always ready to go running to
another study because someone says, "This is where the truth
is, over here." It is time to stop, receive the kingdom, and let
it grow within you.
What is the kingdom of God? It is the reign of God in individual hearts. We see the results when one speaks a kind
word, does a kind deed, is gracious, loving, and understanding in Jesus' name. If you do not wish for the kingdom
of God, do not pray for it. The kingdom will rule your heart
and change the whole course of your life. It may come
silently (it will come, you cannot chase it down), but it will
require openness in love, worship, prayer, and work. "Keep
thy heart with all diligence, for out of it are the issues of life"
(Prov. 4:23, KJV).
Thy kingdom come, not *my* kingdom. My heart has to

open the doors and welcome the Savior, not grudgingly but joyously. Settle down for he is here to stay. I do not have to run chasing after him from one group to another. He has come to my heart's door and I say, "Dear Savior, come in. Let your kingdom fill my heart and soul and life, and let me not grieve you. Guard my heart, my words, and actions. Make me ready for whatever change you may bring into my life as I pray "Thy kingdom come.'"

The result of the power of the kingdom of God in men is made manifest through the church. We *can* pray "Thy kingdom come" as we send missionaries, teach children, comfort the bereaved, pray for the sick, work with prisoners, clothe and feed the unfortunate, give our time, talents, and money to see that all men everywhere have the opportunity to know the beautiful loving grace of God through Jesus Christ.

God's Will

William Barkley says that nothing has done the Christian faith and the church more harm than the blasphemous use of "It is God's will." There are those who go into a home where a child has been killed in an accident or there is someone suffering agony from a disease or some such situation and say, "It is God's will." It is never God's will for a child to be needlessly killed or one to suffer a dread disease. Situations such as these are the direct opposite of the will of God; suffering is the result of the sin of the human situation. Jesus Christ came to defeat pain and sorrow and suffering. His miracles show this.

It may be that we have to take some poignant disappointment or agonizing sacrifice or face something from which our whole being shrinks.

In these times of human agony we have to say: "This is not God's will." This situation is the result, in some way, of the sin and folly of mankind. God did not send it to you. But God can bring you through it still standing on your own two feet. Out of this agony you can become stronger and nearer to God and better able to minister to others than you were before. God can bring good even from things that are outside his will, to those who love and trust him. If you will allow God to use this circumstance and to use you, even this can become part of his will.

When we pray "Thy will be done," it doesn't mean that we expect to be exempt from trouble. The lesson of Jesus in Matthew 26:34-46 is that he was not released but given the power to go through it. We pray not to be taken out of a situation but for strength to face it, conquer it, and defeat it. We pray for triumph. In Daniel 3:16-18 the men did not look for escape, but power to face the situation, whatever the outcome.

To understand God's will for my life I must come to know God and something of his character—what he is like. God, our Father, embodies all the best qualities of father, mother and friend. He plans and provides and desires good and beautiful things for his children. As daily needs arise, we should offer this prayer: "Thy will be done in this matter, Father." Not "Thy will be *endured.*"

God does the best he can with the mess of our lives that we hand him. We choose a certain level of life, and God has to work the best for human lives that can be done through the human will. Our Father must not be blamed for the catastrophes and heartaches we encounter. He does the best thing possible under the circumstances. We can raise our level by being open to God in every area of life; we cannot close the door in special areas. We must use our intelligence and learn through experience. We must pray by thinking logically about the situation and then quietly taking it all to God to learn what his will is for us as individuals. Each life is different and what is good for one may not be good for another.

He Loves Us

When we understand that God through Jesus showed us how he loves us, we can lose our fear of what tomorrow will bring whether it be a disappointment, disease, public humiliation and embarrassment, war, or death. We know we will feel the sting and pain, and he doesn't expect us to like it, but we learn to walk through it without terror knowing that God is with us in the situation leading us through it. God's hands can transform our lives if we can place ourselves wholly in his will. It may take long years of inner growth before we can understand how his will is working out in a given situation.

How can I find God's will?

1. First, cultivate a sensitiveness to the Holy Spirit through prayer, study, and openness of mind and heart.
2. God will guide as we recognize our talents and abilities. (He would not expect one who is tone deaf to direct a choir.)
3. Think *sensibly* in seeking God's will. God will not reverse the moral universe to answer a selfish or immoral whim.
4. *Desire* his will; do not *resign* yourself to his will.
5. True prayer is deliberately putting ourselves at God's disposal and under God's influence.

Day 1

And again Jesus spoke to them in parables, saying, "The kingdom of heaven may be compared to a king who gave a marriage feast for his son, and sent his servants to call those who were invited to the marriage feast; but they would not come. Again he sent other servants, saying, 'Tell those who are invited, Behold, I have made ready my dinner, my oxen and my fat calves are killed, and everything is ready; come to the marriage feast.' But they made light of it and went off, one to his farm, another to his business, while the rest seized his servants, treated them shamefully, and killed them. The king was angry, and he sent his troops and destroyed those murderers and burned their city. Then he said to his servants, 'The wedding is ready, but those invited were not worthy. Go therefore to the thoroughfares, and invite to the marriage feast as many as you find.' And those servants went out into the streets and gathered all whom they found, both bad and good; so the wedding hall was filled with guests (Matt. 22:1-10).

This scripture has taken on new meaning for me in the light of my recent travel experiences. If this passage had a title, it would be "God's Protocol." There is a whole world of diplomatic protocol of which most of us are unaware. Such formality may sound silly and antiquated, but there can be no denying that it exists.

When my husband and I were selected as special ambassadors to represent the President of the United States at the inauguration ceremonies of President William Tolbert of Liberia, West Africa, we felt honored and gladly accepted the privilege and responsibility. As we took part in the week's activities, we were impressed over and over again with the importance of protocol in international affairs. Each nation who maintains an embassy in Liberia sent the ambassador and his wife. Special delegations also represented prominent business concerns. Each ambassador or delegation was assigned seating in order of its rank in importance. Some mistakes or misunderstandings (and there were some) resulted in heated discussions and additional chairs to certain areas. Above all, for a nation to have refused to send a representative would have been an insult too difficult to overcome.

The king in this parable of the kingdom was insulted beyond endurance. The invitations had been sent out (the time was never stated on the first notice); he made careful and elaborate preparations; then he sent out the final summons. Actually what transpired was this: He said, "My son is getting married; you are invited to the feast so be ready when I send for you." This was protocol. He did his part, but the response was an insult.

Dear Father, sometimes the most important events of life slip by us unnoticed. We miss many of the good things you have for us simply because we don't accept the opportunities

*you offer. Each time we refuse to accept a responsibility we
become a little less sensitive to your invitations. Father, forgive
me for insulting you. I do love you. Thy kingdom come in my
life through Jesus. Amen.*

Day 2

Read Matthew 22:1-10.
But they made light of it and went off, one to his farm,
another to his business (v. 5).

When a person is asked to accept a responsibility in the
kingdom work, he is faced squarely with commitment. Life is
full of commitments: job, marriage, children, house payments,
and car payments are just a few. We are prone to take the
invitation to teach a church school class lightly. We forget
God's protocol and say, "Sunday is the only day I have to
rest," or "Sunday is for the family, and we like to go to the
lake (or the mountains) and I owe it to my family," or "We
have to go to visit our parents every Sunday." Now none of
these reasons is bad; in fact, they sound pretty good if you
say them with a sincere look! In our daily living we can
become so involved in making ends meet, cooking three or
four meals a day, driving car pools, and providing advantages
for our children that we completely push aside the invitations
to the kingdom. We settle for good things instead of the best
things. We forget that life is eternal, and we must prepare for
it.

*Dear Father, it hurts when I stop and ask myself, "What
have I done to represent the kingdom of heaven today?" How
can I stop this treadmill? I'm not doing anything bad, but
what am I doing for you? Father, please give me the courage to
stop and get my priorities straightened out—to choose the best
for eternal life instead of good for life here and now. Let me
pray, "Thy kingdom come," and be willing to be the vessel. In
Jesus' name. Amen.*

Day 3

Read Matthew 22:1-10.

The king was angry, and he sent his troops and destroyed those murderers and burned their city (v. 7).

Perhaps this verse seems out of place when talking about a wedding feast. However, when Matthew wrote his gospel, after the death of Jesus, the destruction of Jerusalem by Roman armies already had taken place. Matthew wrote this between A.D. 80 and 90. Jerusalem was destroyed in A.D. 70. Complete disaster had come to the people who would not accept Jesus as the Son of God. Matthew added this comment to emphasize the terrible things that happened to a people who ignored the invitation to the kingdom.

I have a feeling about this verse that is purely personal opinion. I think this bit of commentary that Matthew put in for emphasis can be applied to individuals who seem to constantly have a war raging inside them. You've seen them—maybe you are one sometimes—rebellious, raging, selfish, fighting against all they know to be right. The punishment is in the separation we feel from those who love us. The consequence of rebellion is separation and ultimate destruction. Our human bodies (physical, emotional, and spiritual) can only stand so many battles. When the wounds of rage become so deep, the healing process is very difficult and prolonged. How much joy and peace and fun we miss when we choose to go to war.

Our Heavenly Father, you must be grieved when we tear ourselves apart and forget that you have a plan for us. Heal my wounds and let me be responsive to your invitation. Let me love, not hate; seek your guidance instead of rebelling. Let me be a blessing, not trial to my family and friends. May thy kingdom come in my heart, today! In Jesus' name. Amen.

Day 4

Being asked by the Pharisees when the kingdom of God was coming, he answered them, "The kingdom of God is not coming with signs to be observed; nor will they say, 'Lo, here it is!' or 'There!' for behold, the kingdom of God is in the midst of you [or *with* you]" (Luke 17:20, 21).

The people standing around Jesus had hopes for an earthly kingdom where all their fondest dreams would come true. They were not standing in the midst of the kind of kingdom they had in mind. All they could see around them was sickness, crippled and deformed bodies, men who were guilty of cheating each other, each one preoccupied with his own troubles and too busy to notice the desperation in his neighbor. How could the kingdom of God be here? They expected a utopia.

Jesus tried to teach the people that right there in the midst of all that misery the kingdom of heaven had come. God came to those who were heavy with guilt and misery, and he has the power to change it all. The kingdom of God is where Christ is, and Jesus always lingers in the darkest places in the world.

Dear Father, let me be aware of the dark places around me. Don't let me be blind to the despair and hurt in my family, neighbors, and city. Let me be willing to be used to bring the light of Jesus' love into the dark places. It is frightening to realize that I may be the only representative of your kingdom in the dark crevice of my small realm of influence. Thy kingdom come and dwell in me, dear Father, through Jesus Christ, your son. Amen.

Day 5

For behold, the kingdom of God is in the midst of you [within you] (Luke 17:21b).

The kingdom of God is a mystery. We must never think

of it as a gradual, evolutionary Christianization of the world. This would make the kingdom so elusive and distant that we would lose hope in the midst of our problems—rioting, strikes, wars, drug traffic, terminal cancers, accidents, runaway teenagers and adults, gossipy and ugly attitudes, to name but a few. No, the coming of the kingdom takes place in the middle of the anguish and distress and misery of the world. Helmut Thielicke says, "The greatest mysteries of God are always enacted in the depths; and therefore it is the cry from the depths that always has the great promise" (*Our Heavenly Father*, page 65).

The kingdom of God is the kingdom we represent in the inner city mission; it is the kingdom coming in our love and concern for the mentally ill in our hospitals; it is the kingdom shown through the physical care and human love extended in our medical missions here and overseas; it is the kingdom coming to your neighbor or acquaintance when you sit down and listen, really listen to his bleeding heart. The kingdom of God comes and is expressed through frail human efforts.

Dear Father, when I pray, "Thy kingdom come," I must be ready to allow you to work through my life. It is frightening to realize that I may be the only door to the kingdom ever known by those whose lives I touch. Do not let me fail to reach out to those who are desperate in their misery. Give me the insight to see behind the masks and facades that people erect to cover their agony. The kingdom of God is where Jesus Christ is; so dwell in my heart, Lord Jesus. Amen.

Day 6

The Kingdom of God is within you (Luke 17:21b, TEV).

The kingdom of God is a personal matter. We can pray collectively "Thy kingdom come," but unless the individual pray-er has inner life and vitality, the corporate body of believers is impotent. The only reason "the church" can be called dead is if the individual members have grown cold and hard-hearted. How we as individuals feel about matters concerning the work of God's church reflects in the growth and strength or the impotence and death of our church. If in our heart of hearts we have bitterness toward another race (Black, White, Oriental, Indian, etc.), it shows up in the health of the church and in our witness. If we resent having to support the cause of Christ with our financial resources, it shows in the shrinking Christian influence in a pagan society. When we bear a personal grudge toward a fellow church member, it can become so heavy that we can't carry it and our church responsibilities, so we become bitter and vindictive. These are the sorts of things that can kill a church. "Thy kingdom come" can so fill our hearts with love for God and our fellowman that all who are in our influence reflect that love and warmth.

Dear Father, I do pray for your kingdom to come in my heart and life. Let me be filled with the desire to be used in any way you need me. I want to help bring light and love to the dark places in the world. In Jesus' name. Amen.

Day 7

To another he said, "Follow me." But he said, "Lord, let me first go and bury my father." But he said to him, "Leave the dead to bury their own dead; but as for you, go and proclaim the kingdom of God." Another said, "I will follow you, Lord; but let me first say farewell to those at my home." Jesus said to him, "No one who puts his hand to the plow and looks back is fit for the kingdom of God" (Luke 9:59-62).

Several commentators point out that Jesus was not really as harsh as he sounded when he said, "Let the dead bury their own dead." They suggest that this was very likely the best excuse the man could come up with—his father was probably in very good health. The man had spiritual feelings stirring around in him but failed to take the moment. It is a psycho-

logical fact that if we don't do the good things we feel
compelled to do right then, in all probability we never will do
them.

We don't know much about plowing these days, but it
stands to reason that you can't plow a straight furrow while
looking back over your shoulder. We've all seen people who
got stuck in the glories of college days and never have been
able to mature past the cheerleader/football hero stage.
What's past is past, whether it was good or bad. We can turn
our back on past sins and disappointments and pray
earnestly, "Thy kingdom come in my life today."

*Dear Father, make me fit for thy kingdom. Give me
strength to put behind me all the sins and memories that blot
out your purpose for me. Let me have the courage to look
forward and step out to proclaim the kingdom of God. I am so
prone to put off until tomorrow things I should do now—the
note of appreciation to a teacher, the encouraging word to a
child, a phone call to a sick friend. Help me to stop making
excuses and make way for your kingdom in my life. In Jesus'
name. Amen.*

10

Give Us This Day

Give us this day our daily bread (Matt. 6:11, KJV).

*B*ible scholars find this simple petition very difficult to interpret because of the Greek word used for *daily*. This is the only place in all of Greek literature that this Greek word *epiousios* occurs. The writer probably coined a word that spoke more directly to the people of that day.

We may feel very secure in using the quite simple and obvious meaning of this phrase. It stands alone to speak volumes to us as we stop to meditate on it.

This is a simple petition for the simple, ordinary needs of life. We must acknowledge the proper place of God in our lives and our dependence upon him. We need to feel the comforting fatherly pressure which we miss when we *expect* instead of *ask* for daily needs. Without God there would be no food at all—God gives as man toils. God supplies the soil, sun, rain, and the secret of life while man supplies the work and daily cultivation. Prayer alone will not put food on the table. There may be food in the cupboard, but it has to be prepared and placed on the table. Give *us our* daily bread is a commitment that eliminates selfishness—as we receive, we must also give.

Daily bread teaches us something about anxiety. God taught the children of Israel to be dependent on him for their daily needs. He who created the day provided sustenance for the day (Ex. 16:1-21). Jesus taught that God's care is sufficient to remove all anxiety about our needs (Matt. 6:25-31). We have no time but the immediate. The past is gone, the future must be left in the hands of God. We need not fear the future. Live one day at a time—daily bread.

Day 1

> Behold the fowls of the air: for they sow not, neither do they reap, nor gather into barns; yet your heavenly Father feedeth them. Are ye not much better than they? Therefore take no thought, saying, What shall we eat? or, What shall we drink? or, Wherewithal shall we be clothed? (For after all these things do the Gentiles seek:) for your heavenly Father knoweth that ye have need of all these things (Matt. 6:26, 31, 32, KJV).

For those fortunate people who have never had to worry about having enough money for food, clothing, or shelter this petition may seem a little ridiculous. The young people who were born in the affluence of the Fifties and Sixties will have difficulty understanding the basic human needs. It is hard to understand that a mother or father will resort to stealing food for their starving child if you have never experienced the hunger which comes from the ache and pain of poverty.

Jesus is concerned about our bodies. He spent a lot of time healing ailing bodies and feeding hungry mouths. He cares whether or not we have food to eat, clothes to cover our bodies, and shelter from the elements. Jesus says, "Be not anxious about tomorrow," but for one who has no financial means whatsoever, this is hard to accept.

The next time you ride through a slum area and see the glassy-eyed stares of the unemployed men sitting on the porch steps, the swollen bellies of the children picking through the garbage in the gutters, the flies swarming over the bony old dog slumped in the corner of the yard, remember that Jesus was aware of this human predicament and addressed himself to it when teaching us to pray, "Give *us our* bread." If you are one of the well-fed minority of the world, be thankful and then do something to care for others. They cannot hear the gospel over gnawing, growling stomachs.

Dear Father, bless all those who are hungry and cannot sleep this night. Bless those who are racked with anxiety and pain. Bless those who are far from home and friends. Give them a sense of your love and presence; comfort them in their misery. Father, if there is a way I can minister today, let me be the Christ incarnate for someone. In Jesus' name. Amen.

Day 2

> And, behold, there came a leper and worshiped him, saying Lord, if thou wilt, thou canst make me clean. And Jesus put forth his hand, and touched him, saying, I will; be thou clean. And immediately his leprosy was cleansed (Matt. 8:2-3, KJV).

Jesus is aware of how the problems that beset our bodies can affect our relationship to God and our fellow human beings. Physical disabilities can create great barriers.

Leprosy is a disease that most of us never even think about. When our family visited missionaries in Thailand several years ago, we were brought face to face with the horrors of this deforming disease. In the village of Bankla near the Cambodian border there is a rehabilitation center for lepers on the fringe of the property owned by the Baptist Mission hospital. As we visited with them and saw the beautiful, intricately carved and painted miniature wooden tables, chairs and ships, we were amazed. These people had nubs for arms and legs and were in varying stages of disfigurement. They were not helpless or hopeless. In a country where over two percent of the population can expect to have leprosy they are usually hidden under the house and thrown a little food occasionally or left to wander until overtaken by starvation, the disease, or the elements. These lepers had been treated with love, respect and medicine; and the love and respect had helped as much as the medical care.

We need not hesitate to take our physical ailments, large or small, to our Father. He understands and cares when we are sick. We take our needs and leave them in the hands of

God who loves us dearly. He will give us the things necessary for the day.

*Dear Father, let me not limit my concern and love to my
family and friends. Let me be aware of pain and suffering
throughout the world. Although sometimes my pain is overwhelming, give me strength to overcome it. Strength for today,
Father. Grace for today. In Jesus' name. Amen.*

Day 3

When Gideon heard the telling of the dream and its
interpretation, he worshiped; and he returned to the camp
of Israel, and said, "Arise, for the Lord has given the host
of Midian into your hand" (Judg. 7:15).

One of my daily struggles is with my habit of making
excuses for my actions. Rather than assume the responsibility
for my own mistakes, I have learned to make elaborate
excuses. "I'm late today because someone kept me on the
phone." "I burned the cake because the oven temperature
was set too high." "I didn't get that order because my client
was in a big hurry."

Nothing undercuts effective living more than excuses.
When I allow myself to be manipulated by others, I lose the
power to control my own life. I am responsible for myself,
whether I'm right or wrong. God loves me just like I am. I
have worth in his eyes and he will give me courage to take
the responsibility for my own life.

Power is available to those who are willing to strip themselves of excuses and ask God for power to live honestly and
creatively. Remember the power God gave Gideon and his
three hundred men over the swarms of Midianites? Or the
power of Moses, Deborah, Martin Luther, and other men and
women of God through the years, even today?

*Oh, Father, help me stop making excuses and accept the
power available to me. Let me not weep over lost battles but
look ahead to future opportunities. Thank you for loving me as*

I am, but help me to get my act together so that I can be useful to you and my fellow human beings.

And now, dear Father, I pray that with each day that passes you will deliver me from my sins. Let me daily grow in the knowledge of thee. Bless especially those who are dear to me. Make me thy channel to reach the hearts of those who are troubled today. In Jesus' name. Amen.

Day 4

In the beginning was the Word and the Word was with God, and the Word was God. He was in the beginning with God (John 1:1-2).

Ask and it will be given you; seek, and you will find; knock, and it will be opened to you. For every one who asks receives, and he who seeks finds, and to him who knocks it will be opened (Matt. 7:7-8).

In the beginning was the Word—not the deed, not the feeling. Feelings and actions fade away, but words live on in our minds and on paper for future generations. We must learn to express our deepest longings and feelings to God through words. Words are powerful. Prayer, in the teachings of Jesus, is communication. We not only need to express ourselves to our Father, but we need to be quiet and listen to him speak our name and also to read the words we have preserved for us. They are appropriate throughout all ages.

The Father says, "Cast all your anxieties on me." "Ask, seek, knock." That means that when we experience the crises of life—death of a loved one, frustrations with children, illness, etc.—we can ask, seek, knock, and cast our burdens before the Lord. The gift of our Father is the fellowship that fills our souls. We learn to walk in fellowship with our Father, maybe still unsure of the future, but secure in his loving care. Our life here is not all there is—only in heaven can we know in full.

Let us make this prayer of St. Augustine ours for today:

"Grant me, even me, dearest Lord, to know Thee and love Thee and rejoice in Thee. And, if I cannot do these perfectly in this life, let me at least advance to higher degrees every day, till I can come to do them in perfection. Let the knowledge of Thee increase in me here, that it may be full hereafter. Let the love of Thee grow every day more and more here, that it may be perfect hereafter; that my joy may be great in itself, and full in Thee. I know, O God, that Thou are a God of truth; make good Thy gracious promises to me, that my joy may be full." In Jesus' name. Amen.

Day 5

And in praying do not heap up empty phrases as the Gentiles do; for they think that they will be heard for their many words. Do not be like them, for your Father knows what you need before you ask him. Pray then like this: Our Father who art in heaven, . . . Give us this day our daily bread (Matt. 6:7-9).

How much do you really know about yourself? Do you know yourself in the inner person well enough to know what is best for you in every circumstance? For a week or so try keeping a daily diary of the things you pray for—just jot them down briefly. It may read something like this: (1) Don't let me fail that test. (2) Let him ask me for a date. (3) Don't let the boss be mad at me today. (4) Let my child stay off drugs and alcohol. (5) Give me strength for today, etc. After a week go back and read them and see if they make sense to you. If not, put yourself in God's hands; learn more about yourself; become a more perceptive person; turn your thoughts outward; become a loving, helping person—not a tense, tight, demanding, grasping drone.

So often we pray for senseless things that have no relation to our needs. Learn to know yourself so that you may pray more effectively. But even so we don't have to depend on our limited abilities. God knows us, he knew us before the foundation of the earth. He will fill in all the corners and crevices because he is always there before we pray. "Your

Father knows what you need before you ask him." If we are not retrospective, sensitive, and open about ourselves and others, we may never even know when, how or if God answers our prayers.

Dear Heavenly Father, we want to be liberated—free! We forget that freedom comes from within. Maybe this selfishness, my mean boss, the cranky neighbor, my grouchy husband is really reflecting me. Free me from these bad attitudes. Father, you know what I need. Take my words, actions, intentions, thoughts, and by your blessing let them be pleasing in your sight. Through Jesus Christ, your precious son. Amen.

Day 6

> The Lord is my shepherd, I shall not want; he makes me lie down in green pastures. He leads me beside still waters; he restores my soul (Ps. 23:1, 2).

The psalmist knew about the "dailyness" of life. Just keeping life together is sometimes almost impossible. The pieces slip through our fingers, and in spite of all we do, they break into seemingly impossible fragments. Maybe you're a teenager about to be on your own, and you're admitting to yourself that you're scared. Maybe you are in the midst of a floundering marriage, or your business is bankrupt. Maybe you are facing serious illness, and you don't know the outcome. Perhaps you are having to carry burdens not only for yourself but for several families. Daily bread takes care of all our needs. Here is where we focus in on what we personally need to get us through the hours and days. Don't be ashamed to bring the festering sore, the heartbreak, the parent, the child or you, yourself, to our Father.

The psalmist felt God's guidance as a shepherd watchfully caring for his sheep—always providing for the needs. "He restores my soul." Your "still waters" may be this time of prayer you have set aside. He *will* restore your soul.

Our Heavenly Father, please be in this situation with me.

Give me strength to handle any situation I may confront today. Father, I need help today. Be my shepherd and restore my soul. In Jesus' precious name. Amen.

Day 7

When I consider thy heavens, the work of thy fingers, the moon and the stars, which thou hast ordained; what is man, that thou art mindful of him? And the son of man, that thou visitest him? (Ps. 8:3, 4, KJV).

To the psalmist who could see only a few stars in comparison to those we can see today, it seemed almost unbelievable that God could be aware of him. The vastness of the universe, the masses of human beings make us wonder how God can possibly know about me, about you.

Not long ago I saw thousands of people who were wanting so desperately to be known individually by God. We were in the large Buddhist temple in the center of bustling, throbbing Taipei, Taiwan. Everywhere people of all ages were burning incense and bowing and offering prayers to the cold, hard, nonseeing Buddha. At the altar was a mother with a little girl not more than two or three years old. The mother made the child kneel and kept pushing her head down in a bowing motion. If only this mother and child could know the love so amazing—the love that encompasses all people everywhere.

One of the daily needs we have is to be loved and known by our heavenly Father. It is desolate to be alone *and* lonely. God is mindful of each of his children.

Dear Heavenly Father, I am so small and insignificant. The world is so vast. Thank you for not being limited by my ability to understand. Thank you for picking me out of the masses; thank you for loving me in my loneliness. Let me pray as did St. Augustine, "Grant me, even me, dearest Lord, to know Thee and love Thee." In Jesus' name. Amen.

11

Forgive Us Our Debts

And forgive us our debts, As we also have forgiven our debtors (Matt. 6:12).

And forgive us our sins, for we ourselves forgive every one who is indebted to us (Luke 11:4).

*T*here is a simple reason for the difference in the use of words in the Gospels of Matthew and Luke. Both *debts* and *sins* come from the same Aramaic word, *choba*, which literally means "a debt" but is a common rabbinic word for sin. Matthew chose the more Jewish meaning while Luke used a more general Greek word for sin. Tyndale inserted *trespasses* in his translation probably on the basis of the use of the word in Matthew 6:14, 15 when Jesus amplifies his discussion on forgiving. (The word *trespasses* is used only in ancient translations by William Tyndale and later by John Knox.) Most of us skip by this petition very quickly. We are not guilty of murder, robbery, adultery or any of the blatant, really terrible sins. We are God-fearing, law-abiding citizens, and we live decent, respectable lives. So what is there to ask God to forgive? It may be the worst sin not to be aware of any sin at all.

The New Testament uses five different words for sin. Here are their meanings: (1) Missing the target—that is, failing to be what we are capable of being. Could you be a better plumber, or a better lawyer, doctor, mother, father, son or daughter, etc.? (2) There is a line between what is right and wrong. Are you always on the right side which divides truth from falsehood; are you kind or harsh; do you let a look or facial expression deny your words? (3) A slipping, sliding fall into impulsive or passionate sinfulness—losing self-control. (4) Doing what one pleases regardless of the law or the outcome—knowing what is right, yet defiantly doing what is wrong. (5) Failing to pay what is due. Duty to God and fellowman can never be completely fulfilled.

"Since all have sinned and fall short of the glory of God" (Rom. 3:23). The Bible is never afraid to show its great men under the conviction of sin. There was Simon Peter (Luke 5:8), all Christians (1 John 1:10), the young seeker (Matt. 19:16-22), the ruler (Luke 18:18-23), Paul (1 Tim. 1:15), a good man (Mark 10:17-22), and David (Psalm 38:18), to mention a few. The Bible also shows the national sinfulness of people and the consequences: Sodom and Gomorrah in Genesis 18 and 19; 2 Peter 2:5-8; the children of Israel in Exodus 16:8, 32:31; and Babylon in Jeremiah 51:6, 13:52. Do not dare pray this petition unless you can forgive, because you become your own judge. "Forgive us our sins *in proportion* as we forgive our debtors."

Jesus teaches that in order to be forgiven we must be forgiving. He who forgives will find for himself the forgiveness of God. Read these scriptures: Matthew 6:14-15; Matthew 18:23-25; Matthew 7:1, 2; James 2:13; Mark 4:24; and Luke 6:37-38.

This petition is crucial to the Christian life. It is amazing how situations and attitudes can change when they are prayed about in a genuine spirit of forgiveness. If you have a bad situation in your office you can usually trace the source of that problem to an individual who is very unhappy. Perhaps that person is really sending signals asking for help. Pray for that person sincerely and before long you will see a difference. It may be that the difference is in the way you react to him; and hopefully he will change, also. Prayer can change the attitude you have toward people and situations.

One of the questions that people ask about this petition is: How do I know when I have really forgiven someone? This is difficult because forgiveness does not come instantly where there has been a deep wound. From the human side, we must keep praying about it. Every day continue to pray for the person who has hurt you so deeply. One day when you see that person or even hear that person's voice you'll realize all of a sudden that you don't have that knot of hatred anymore. You can see them and that grudge won't be the first thing you think of. The process of forgiving is gradual in many instances.

A very dear older friend told me of a situation that occurred in her life as a young mother. Someone whom she had considered a good friend had spread some very nasty gossip about her, and she was heartbroken and hurt and angry. For a long time she prayed very hard about this because she didn't like the way it made her feel. Many months went by and one summer day she was busy caring for her baby when this friend who had hurt her so badly called her name at the front door. Before she realized it, she recognized her voice and called out, "Come on in, I'm so glad to see you!" And to her own surprise she really was glad! The wound had healed through forgiveness, leaving a scar that dimmed with time. If she had nurtured and kept alive her hurt and anger it would have grown bigger and distorted her whole view of life. Fostering hatred for people can cause all sorts of physical problems like severe headache, stomach upset, and even ulcers. What a pity we don't practice the healing art of forgiveness.

Another form of forgiveness concerns our feelings about ourselves. This forgiveness has to do with words such as *grace, acceptance, sin, despair*, and *guilt*. Is there anyone who does not know that vast, uneasy, groping feeling in the pit of the stomach that ultimately spells separation? Three areas of separation occur in every life: separation from our fellow beings; separation of "me from myself"; and separation of man (individual and collective) from God. Sin and grace are hard to define, but because we know that "*all* have sinned," God provides grace (acceptance and forgiveness) for us, his children.

Learn to forgive and then *forget*. Do not brood over a hurt or injury because this becomes a grudge. There is always a reason why someone does something. You may never know why, or it may not make sense. Learn to understand and forget or you may become bitter and harsh. Paul says, "Be kind to one another, tenderhearted, forgiving one another, as God in Christ forgave you" (Eph. 4:32).

Day 1

> For if you forgive men their trespasses, your heavenly Father also will forgive you; but if you do not forgive men their trespasses, neither will your Father forgive your trespasses (Matt. 6:14-15).

This is the only petition that Jesus explained. Obviously it is the door of God's kingdom. He could not have put it any plainer or any more positive than this. He doesn't say, "If you sin"; it is a foregone conclusion that we will all sin and stand in need of forgiveness. So often the sequence of events is like a row of blocks—one falls and knocks the next one down and so on down the line. It's like when Dad comes home unhappy and yells at Mom; Mom screams at big brother; brother hits sister; sister hits the dog; and the dog bites the cat, etc. Not only can this poisonous atmosphere of returning evil for evil settle on a home; it can infect a nation and the whole world. The cry for vengeance is heard all over the world. Reconciliation is a hard commodity to achieve. Retaliation is much easier; we just keep generating it back and forth.

Jesus did not say for us to pray for revenge for our debtors. He presupposes that we need to seek forgiveness; so first, be forgiving.

Dear Father, grant me thy forgiveness. Wipe the slate clean with your holiness. Forgive any evil thoughts or actions, forgive any pain or anguish I may have caused. Father, teach me to be forgiving toward those with whom I had differences today. Give me courage and strength to acknowledge this to them. Let me be generous with forgiveness. In the name of Jesus who prayed for me from the cross in agony, "Forgive them, Father." Amen.

Day 2

So if you are offering your gift at the altar, and there remember that your brother has something against you, leave your gift there before the altar and go; first be reconciled to your brother, and then come and offer your gift (Matt. 5:23-24).

A man is never closer and more like God than when he forgives a fellowman. Jesus sets it out right here very clearly. It is obvious how important this forgiveness is—as we said earlier, the very door to the kingdom. This makes no sense to one who is not a disciple of Jesus Christ. I first must have a relationship to God and see the world, my country, my neighbor through his eyes. If I can see them as he sees them, their appearance is totally different and it also changes my conduct.

You may be thinking, "I don't know that I have anything against anyone." Is there someone with whom you have had disagreement? Is there someone who may *think* that you have done them wrong—perhaps they didn't understand your motives? Even if you are right and they are wrong, it is up to you to make it right on your part.

This petition brings us to the point of being Godlike. If you can forgive, your whole life will have a different tone.

Dear Father, teach me, help me to really be able to forgive those who wrong me and with whom I disagree. Help me clear the channels of my relationships with people so that I may have full fellowship with you. In Jesus' name. Amen.

Day 3

> Blessed is he whose transgression is forgiven, whose
> sin is covered. Blessed is the man to whom the Lord
> imputes no iniquity, and in whose spirit there is no deceit.
> When I declared not my sin, my body wasted away
> through my groaning all day long. For day and night thy
> hand was heavy upon me; my strength was dried up as by
> the heat of summer. I acknowledged my sin to thee, and I
> did not hide my iniquity; I said, "I will confess my trans-
> gressions to the Lord"; then thou didst forgive the guilt of
> my sin (Ps. 32:1-5).

Remember when you were a child and you did something
you knew was wrong, and you were so afraid your mother
would find out about it. Then when bedtime came you tried
to sleep, but you were so miserable. Finally, when mother
brought your third glass of water, you blurted out a confession and burst into tears. Remember how she took you in her
arms, spoke soothingly, and all was forgiven? It was over. You
didn't have to carry that weight anymore, and undisturbed
sleep came.

It is dreadful to have to carry around the burden of sin.
As the psalmist says, "Day and night thy hand was heavy
upon me." Then later he says, "Be glad in the Lord, and
rejoice, . . . shout for joy" (Ps. 32:11).

*Dear Father, thank you for the gift of forgiveness. Let me
never add to another person's burden by failing to forgive
them. Forgiveness brings release and joy. Forgiveness can
release the stranglehold of guilt. I lay it all before you, Father.
In the name of Jesus who prayed for the forgiveness of his
murderers. Amen.*

Day 4

> Then Peter came up and said to him, "Lord, how often
> shall my brother sin against me, and I forgive him? As
> many as seven times?" Jesus said to him, "I do not say to

you seven times, but seventy times seven" (Matt. 18:21-22).

Peter sounded much like most of us today. We feel that we are not really in danger of falling into sin. We become arrogant and assume that the problem lies with someone else. "It's not my fault" is a commonly used phrase. We are much quicker to see the faults of others than to discern our own inadequacies. We can always say that we were misunderstood or misinformed to avoid assuming responsibility for the pain around us.

Remember when you bombarded your neighbor with harsh words because your children were having a disagreement? Or her dog ruined your favorite azalea? Remember when you were afraid to ask your friend about her problems? You just talked and talked and ignored her bleeding heart. Maybe you couldn't handle it, but all she needed was for someone to listen or just acknowledge her pain. How about the young man who came to your church, dressed well but with very long hair. Did your sneer shut him out and turn him off? How about the man or woman who has the desk next to yours and is crying out for attention in an obnoxious way? What is your reaction? Have you drawn a circle of isolation around your life so you won't be "tarnished"? How many times shall I forgive my brother?

Father, forgive me, please. I have thoughtlessly created wounds. Let me heal. Forgive me as I forgive others. Keep me aware of this responsibility. Let forgiveness set the tone of my life. In the name of Jesus who taught us how to forgive. Amen.

Day 5

Read all of Psalm 103. These verses are a portion of this beautiful song of David: Bless the Lord . . . who forgives all your iniquity [sins], who heals all your diseases, . . . He does not deal with us according to our sins, . . . as far as the east is from the west, so far does he remove our transgressions from us. . . . Bless the Lord, O my soul!

When God forgives us, he forgives completely! We don't have to worry about our sins being forever paraded before us. He is not like a woman I heard about. Her husband had been unfaithful but had repented—asked forgiveness, and she allowed him to come home. She took him back, but they never knew any joy in their relationship again. She became so caustic and bitter that the man never knew any peace.

When we repent and ask forgiveness, God puts our sins away forever. The blood of Jesus has covered them. Yes, there may be scars from the wounds inflicted, but God forgives and wipes the slate clean so we can go on with the guilt lifted and joy in our soul again.

Thank you, dear Father, for understanding us and for not dealing with us forever about our sins. We don't deserve it but we are grateful for your loving, free forgiveness. Now please give us the ability and grace to do the same for our fellow beings. Bless the Lord, O my soul. In Jesus' name. Amen.

Day 6

And in anger his lord delivered him to the jailers, till he should pay all his debt. So also my heavenly Father will do to every one of you, if you do not forgive your brother from your heart (Matt. 18:34-35).

This is the end of a parable Jesus told to illustrate the answer he gave Peter concerning how much and how often he should forgive his brother. Begin with verse 23 and read the whole story. In summary, it speaks of a man who owes a vast amount to his landlord. In today's language he would have to declare bankruptcy. He pled his case and the landlord was kindhearted and generous and forgave him the whole debt. The man walked out, free and clear, and on his way home met a friend who owed him about twenty dollars. He literally seized the man by the throat and demanded his money. The poor man simply didn't have it and begged for more time, but our villain had him thrown in prison. When word of this spread throughout the community, the landlord was furious. "I forgave you all that debt and you didn't even have half as much mercy on you friend as I had on you." And he threw him in jail till he could pay his debt in full.

The lesson is clear. God is so gracious in forgiving all of our sinfulness. We can't be bad enough for God to deny us. And yet, we are so grudging and stingy with our forgiveness to our fellow human beings. Forgive from the *heart.* As you forgive, God will forgive you!

Heavenly Father, teach me daily to forgive. Help me portray a spirit of kindness to all I touch. I am not without the need of forgiveness—keep me ever mindful of that need. In Jesus' name. Amen.

Day 7

None of the transgressions which he has committed shall be remembered against him; for the righteousness which he has done he shall live (Ezek. 18:22).

Isn't it wonderful to know that God says, "I will remember their sin no more"? Then he goes on to add, "I will only remember the good things." When the roll call of the faithful is given, we can be sure that only the good things will be listed beside our names.

Look at the eleventh chapter of Hebrews. Noah is praised and not a word of his sin mentioned; Abraham is praised with no mention of his lying about Sarah; Sarah is praised and not a word of her laughing at God. Isn't that like God? Now this is the point where God demands that we be like him. Forgive one who has wrongfully used you and find something good to remember about that person. Replace evil with good.

Also, it is best to keep your disagreement or hurt only between you and the one involved. Don't tell the world or even one other person about it. "If your brother sins against you, go and tell him his fault, between you and him *alone*"

(Matt. 18:15). It will be easier to handle without a lot of other people giving advice.

Just remember that when God takes sin away, he takes it so far away that it cannot be found—it is forgotten.

Father, thank you for your marvelous forgiveness. Let me grow a sweet spirit; let me also not only forgive but forget. Heal the wounded souls and give us peace in our lives. In Jesus' name. Amen.

12

Lead Us Not Into Temptation

And lead us not into temptation, but deliver us from evil (Matt. 6:13).

We are constantly hounded and bombarded by perils and pitfalls. The pressure is so great that we may be torn away from our Father and succumb to "other gods." Helmut Thielicke says that perhaps we should say, "Let nothing become a temptation to me" (*Our Heavenly Father*, Harper & Row, p. 121). Our most cherished possessions can get between us and the Father—home, husband, wife, child, parent, job, school, etc. Fears concerning that which could be lost can separate us from God—loss of reputation, loss of position, loss of family. Things that consume our time and attention can separate us from God—television, recreation, anything that removes us from the place of worship on Sunday.

Sin is anything that separates one from God. High and grand ideas sometimes are our downfall. We can be so intoxicated with good deeds and ambitions that we are astounded and impressed with success. We lose all perspective. God knows that we face temptations. Even Jesus was tempted, as we are, with something glorious, pleasurable, interesting and powerful.

The word *tempt* carries the meaning for test. Temptation or testing is not designed to make us fall but to make us strong. Testing makes a person stronger and better able to

cope with life. No man can be used by God until he has been
tested and tried. This testing builds character. "Lead us not
into temptation" gives the idea that even though all men must
be tested (tempted) we pray that we will not be left in the
power and control of temptation. "When temptation does
come, do not abandon me, Lord."

Read the following Scriptures about temptation: Jesus was
tested by Satan (Matt. 4:1-11); Jesus admonishing his disciples
(Matt. 26:41); Jesus and Satan (Luke 4:13, 14); Fair-weather
believers (Luke 8:13); God is faithful (1 Cor. 10:13); Simon
Peter was sifted as wheat (Luke 22:31, 32); Stand the test and
receive a crown of life (James 1:12-15); and God will receive
you (2 Peter 2:9).

There is never any doubt in the Bible that there is an
active, personal power in direct opposition to God. Several
terms are used for this competitor for men's souls—Devil,
Tempter, Satan, Adversary, Evil One, Beelzebul, and Prince of
Darkness. Satan stands for everything that is anti-man and
anti-God. This phrase, "Deliver us from evil," frankly
acknowledges the dangers of the human situation and
confesses our inadequacy to deal with it. We deliver
ourselves, the danger and our weaknesses, to the protecting
power of God. With our hand in the loving, caring, protecting
hand of God we need not squabble with the powers of evil
nor fear the "ordeal" of the journey of life. He takes care of
us. Jesus himself teaches us to pray this prayer and he
assumes the responsibility that the prayer will be heard. He
does help those who trust him with everything—family,
fortune, reputation. God never lets a person down. He hears
and walks beside us. "For we have not a great high priest
who is unable to sympathize with our weaknesses, but one
who in every respect has been tempted as we are, yet without
sin" (Heb. 4:15). Helmut Thielicke says, "He is not only the
Lord who hears but also the Brother who bears our burdens
with us" (Ibid., p. 129).

In this verse there is also a message for the church. The
church must be the bulwark of strength, the lighthouse to

show the way, to give strength to the weak, to shed light in the darkest places and preach the gospel of Jesus Christ. The church must offer comfort and love to the sinful, sorrowful souls of men. As angels ministered to Jesus, so the church must ever be ready to minister in the Gethsemanes of human pain and anguish.

Day 1

So God created man in his own image, in the image of God he created him; male and female he created them. And God blessed them, and God said to them, "Be fruitful and multiply, and fill the earth and subdue it, and have dominion over the fish of the sea and over the birds of the air and over every living thing that moves upon the earth." And God said, "Behold, I have given you every plant yielding seed which is upon the face of all the earth, and every tree with seed in its fruit; you shall have them for food. And to every beast of the earth, and to every bird of the air, and to everything that creeps on the earth, every-thing that has the breath of life, I have given every green plant for food." And it was so. And God saw everything that he had made, and behold, it was very good. And there was evening and there was morning, the sixth day (Gen. 1:27-31).

And they heard the sound of the Lord God walking in the garden in the cool of the day, and the man and his wife hid themselves from the presence of the Lord God among the trees of the garden. But the Lord God called to the man, and said to him, "Where are you?" And he said, "I heard the sound of thee in the garden, and I was afraid, because I was naked; and I hid myself" (Gen. 3:8-10).

How loving and caring our Father is! Humanity without God, the Father, would be like delivering a writhing, screaming, frightened baby and then dumping it in a basket to cry pitifully and be left to the terrifying emptiness and loneliness of the dark world.

Our Father created us and then provided us with his unmatched care and love, and yet what happened? Did mankind disobey the Father because there was lack of love, or understanding, or communion between them? Was it because they lacked food or shelter? Was the Father too strict (after all, he told them not to eat the fruit of one tree), or was he too lenient? The Father must have done something wrong for his children to turn out this way. Well, perhaps, he did— he made his family creation with a marvelous mind and overwhelming curiosity, and with a determination and freedom to choose. His mistake was to make us more than puppets on a string. Puppets are entertaining for a short time but would be awfully boring in a lasting relationship. There is no communication; no relationship at all. Where did God go wrong?

I believe that the rift that runs through the world—the blackness, the persecution, the loneliness and helplessness that cuts and tortures the world—was created when God the Father saw his precious children, into whom he had breathed a living soul, in rebellion. His heart was broken. Our Father's being began to ache; he shuddered to feel the pain that would be inflicted on all his children. At that moment the loving, creating, paternal Father began his plan to redeem his rebellious children.

Father in heaven, where did I as a parent go wrong? Why is my child rebelling? My love for my child is exceeded only by your infinite love for all of us. Your heart is also wrung out and broken—for all of your children in rebellion, including me. Thank you for being with me. I need you in this time of testing. In Jesus' holy name. Amen.

Day 2

Your iniquities have made a separation between you and your God, and your sins have hid his face from you (Isa. 59:2).

What one of us has never been a defiant, foot stomping, tantrum throwing child? Can you honestly say, "I would never do anything to displease either my earthly parents or my heavenly Father?" In each person there is that moment of rebellion, a personal experience of having the garden gates closed, and we think we are superior to God's way. We are drawn by our own sinfulness into the magnetic field of decay and disorder. The very fact of our arrogance and selfishness makes it necessary for God to allow this sign of his broken heart, the bleeding wound, to hang over the universe. The rift includes all hostile forces such as death, sickness, suffering, war, etc., which are unnatural powers that broke into God's creation plan when his children first rebelled. The perfect world, the beautiful garden, was rejected just as each person has at some point turned away from the Father and the family.

Jesus himself had to deal with this in the death of his friend Lazarus. His reaction was like ours when we stand by the deathbed of our friends—he was angry that the dark powers should be able to break into God's world. Jesus wept openly. Sickness, suffering, and death are signs that even man's body (made in God's own image) has been pulled into the rift, the chasm that will break us all in two.

Dear Father, thank you for sending Jesus, your only Son, to teach us how to deal with the living of each day. He experienced extreme fatigue, anger and grief over the death of his friend Lazarus, disappointment in his closest friends and chosen companions, and humiliation, to mention only a few. Thank you for letting Jesus teach us the ways of having constant communion with the heavenly Father. He really is calling my name, and I can answer, "Abba, Father!" In Jesus' name. Amen.

Day 3

My God, my God, why hast thou forsaken me? Why art thou so far from helping me, from the words of my groaning? O my God, I cry by day, but thou dost not answer; and by night, but find no rest (Ps. 22:1-2).

Why, Father, have you sent this cancer on me? Why, Father, did you let that accident ruin my legs? Why does my child have leukemia? Why does my friend, a minister's wife, have terminal cancer? She has three children to care for. Why, Father? It isn't fair for innocent people to be so hurt and battered.

We must not say that God sends death or God sends anything bad on us. But even when we do blame God for our misfortunes, he hears and understands the anguish through which we vent our feelings. Evil things are not in the plan of God's creation, but blows and disasters that come to us do not pass unnoticed by God. He knows what is going on, and this is why he provided the life, death, and resurrection of his Son Jesus to be our intermediary—our brother pleading for us before the Father.

The fact that Jesus teaches us this prayer assures us that there is a Father who is at work in the world, taking the mess and transforming our lives through all the troubles. The question turns to us: "What does God have for me?" I must listen for his voice as he calls me through the storm and rage, and answer, "Abba, Father!"

Dear Father, how we fuss and scream at you because we see and experience the powers of evil in our lives. Forgive us, and help us to hear your voice and answer, "Abba, Father!" Everything will be all right because you will give us the ability and grace to take the hard blows. Help us to know that you will take the evil and make it good somehow, if we wait and listen and are open. Let me not fail you. In Jesus' name. Amen.

Day 4

Out of the depths I cry to thee, O Lord! Lord, hear my voice! Let thy ears be attentive to the voice of my supplications! (Ps. 130:1-2).

In July of 1970 my family and I stepped off the plane in almost complete darkness in Bangkok, Thailand. There were armed guards everywhere, and because of the war in Cambodia there was almost a complete blackout. We didn't understand a word being spoken, the heat and odors were overwhelming, and we sort of huddled together wishing for a familiar face. Then we heard the greatest sound in the world. Someone was calling, "Bill! Bill! Look up here! I'll be waiting for you at the other end of customs!" We knew it was our missionary friend, John Patton, who had come to meet us and be our guide through a strange land. Relief and gratitude filled our hearts.

Out in this dark, scary night of our lives somebody is there calling us by name. We don't need to ask, "Who's there?" We know that Jesus walked through Bethlehem, Golgotha, and the open grave so that we do not have to grope through the darkness. He is the one who is there in the night calling us by name, leading us to the Father.

Heavenly Father, our lives are full of dark, scary nights; morning seems so far away. We join the psalmist and pray in his tone, "When the righteous cry for help, the Lord hears, and delivers them out of all their troubles. The Lord is near to the brokenhearted, and saves the crushed in spirit." You, heavenly Father, are the one who walks the dark hallways of my life and calls my name. I know that everything is all right. In Jesus' name. Amen.

Day 5

No temptation has overtaken you that is not common to man. God is faithful, and he will not let you be tempted beyond your strength, but with the temptation will also provide the way of escape, that you may be able to endure it (1 Cor. 10:13).

No temptation has overtaken you that is not common to

man! That is hard to accept when we feel like we must be the special target of the devil. God is faithful. He will not leave us to fight off the evil one alone. There are times when we choose to fight the battle alone and that is when we seem to be swallowed up in our own messy little battlefields.

Those times when we feel that we are being tested and stretched beyond endurance are so terrifying that we want to scream at God, "I've had enough!" Just at the breaking point the way of escape comes, and we have endured it.

An athlete never really knows how good he is until he enters competition. When he has to push himself beyond endurance against his competitor, he is able to measure his strength and endurance. If he never allows himself to measure his abilities, he never knows if he is really any good at all. That's the way it is with our spiritual lives. Until we are pushed and measured we don't know what we can stand. Our bland milk diet is no good for the stiff competition of life. We must strengthen our spiritual armament. We must become strong like iron so that the little tests will be no problem and we will be prepared to muster all our resources when the big competition comes—and it will!

Our Father, we live in such a frightening world. Some days it seems like we'll be eaten alive by all the evil that bombards us. It is so hard to be prepared to meet each situation with the right words and attitude. Are you sure that all the things that happen to me and my family are common to man? Help me to be strong and to endure. Thank you for being faithful to me through everything. In Jesus' name. Amen.

Day 6

> Count it all joy, my brethren, when you meet various
> trials, for you know that the testing of your faith produces
> steadfastness (James 1:2, 3).

Do you ever feel like you awaken each morning to the sounds of battle already stirring? There are smoldering fires

left as reminders of yesterday's skirmishes, and who knows
how the battle will go today or what new conflict will arise?
Only you know what the testings and conflicts in your life
are. For some it is the burning desire to please your peers, to
have the approval of friends; it may be an inordinate desire
for money or fame; it could be backbiting or envy; it could
be lack of patience with children or students; or the overwhelming burden of concern for a loved one. Each of us has
enough personal conflicts to fill a book. I think many times
when we see people sailing along without any obvious
bumps in the way, we assume that they have no problems. I
firmly believe that the more we seek to be in God's will, the
more we recognize the trials and actually do battle between
a wrong desire and a right one. We are ready to do battle
when we say with the psalmist, "Lord, all my desire is before
thee." The aim of testing is to cleanse us of all impurity, to
burn out the dross of human character and make us fit for
God's use. Testing produces unswerving constancy. How can
you know a person is dependable unless you have seen him
under fire? Can God depend on you?

Ask God for strength and help. He gives freely, liberally
to all men without "throwing it up to us." He graciously gives
wisdom for dealing with the trials of life to all who ask
believing that God is powerful and able to handle even our
problems. James tells us to use the experiences of life to
develop a beautiful character. Then he says we must seek for
wisdom from God who will give generously that which is
good and right for us.

*Dear Father, take my desires and make them fit for your
use. Cleanse my life of impurity, of hatred, ill will, the unforgiving spirit. Let me be steadfast for thee. In the name of Jesus.
Amen.*

Day 7

Do not speak evil against one another, brethren. He
that speaks evil against a brother or judges his brother,

speaks evil against the law and judges the law. . . . But who are you that you judge your neighbor? (James 4:11, 12)

You do not know about tomorrow. What is your life? For you are a mist that appears for a little time and then vanishes (James 4:14).

Those who approach God most frequently live closest to him and find it easiest to resist the devil. James was talking to anyone who lives away from God. "All have sinned and fall short of the glory of God" (Rom. 3:23). We need a deepening consciousness of what God demands. Our words, deeds, emotions, and thoughts should all be cleansed. James is demanding that those who are self-satisfied, complacent, easy-going, and unaware of their sins wake up and become conscious of their sins and the sorrows and needs of the world.

It is time for aware, caring Christians to call for reform in our local, state and federal governments. It is shameful for us to stand by impotent to speak out against the sin centers which have invaded even the small towns. It is time for us to cry out, "Draw near unto God and he will draw near to you. Cleanse and purify yourself before God."

Our future is in the hands of God. We must not fear what tomorrow may bring but put all our plans for the future into his hands.

We should never think that we can wait to do the good things. The opportunity may never come again. Read again Matthew 25:35-46. We will be held accountable for the sins of omission. Don't fail to recognize and see opportunities of service—beginning with kind words at home for the family.

Dear Father, we pray for our desires and goals to be God-centered and not self-centered. May we be careful not to judge others. Deliver us from the pitfalls of unconcern and complacency. Let us be ready for your service, beginning at home. Let Jesus' name be holy in my life. Amen.

13

For Thine Is the Kingdom

For thine is the kingdom, and the power, and the glory, for ever. Amen (Matthew 6:13, KJV).

Y ou will note that in the newer translations this final statement of praise is not included. This is because it was not part of the original prayer as is shown by studying the earliest and best manuscripts. Actually it was used by the congregation as a response to the prayer. It became a part of the worship of the church. Since men first began to use this prayer in public, this has been the response of the worshipers. There is substantial biblical evidence for this practice going back to the prayer of David as he prepared for the Temple which his son Solomon would build (1 Chron. 29:11; Ps. 145:11-13).

There is great value in this conclusion to the Lord's Prayer because it gives us the proper perspective of the eternal ways of God—that God is all powerful. It reminds us of the One *to whom* we have been praying.

1. God is king. This prayer is our submission to his authority. We pledge our obedience and allegiance to him.
2. God has heard us, he loves us, and he has the power to act—of this we are confident.
3. Glory belongs to God alone because it is divine. Whatever happens is to glorify God.

4. We remember that our Father has us in his care. Not only is he all powerful but he loves, cares for, and protects his children. We praise him.

This last phrase can be considered a doxology—"Praise God from whom *all* blessings flow." Do you feel completely unraveled, at your wit's end? Are you ever plunged to the depths of despair? Maybe it will lift your soul to put aside your grievances, even the petitions, and simply *praise* God. "For thine is the kingdom, and the power, and the glory, for ever." It can lift the soul above the spell of terror and enable us to see the *eternal* God who is not bound by our time schedule. We know that the kingdom of God is where we will sing the eternal praises.

Day 1

We think of God as loving, listening and powerful to *act.* We can be confident that in his love he has heard, and in his power he will answer.

Glory is a hard word to define. The glory of God is manifest in the beauty of our changing nature (colorful leaves in the fall, the flowers, the blossoming of spring), and also in the marvelous way God uses human lives. This is when the kingdom of God is in the hearts of individuals. Then life is glorious and powerful.

Praising God is to see things from God's point of view. This means that we see things from the perspective of history. This enables us to minister to others even in *our* darkest hours—to sing as Paul did in prison at midnight. Nothing can change us so much as praising God in the worst of times, in life's darkest moments.

This is a doxology, a culmination of worship, an expression of the overflow from the heart of the worshiper. Praise God from whom all blessings flow! Amen.

Day 2

You will say in that day: "I will give thanks to thee, O

Lord, for though thou wast angry with me, thy anger turned away, and thou didst comfort me. Behold God is my salvation; I will trust, and will not be afraid; for the Lord God is my strength and my song, and he has become my salvation." With joy you will draw water from the wells of salvation. And you will say in that day: "Give thanks to the Lord, call upon his name; make known his deeds among the nations, proclaim that his name is exalted. Sing praises to the Lord, for he has done gloriously, let this be known in all the earth. Shout, and sing for joy, O inhabitant of Zion, for great in your midst is the Holy One of Israel" (Isaiah 12).

Day 3

"Turn to me and be saved, all the ends of the earth! For I am God, and there is no other. By myself I have sworn, from my mouth has gone forth in righteousness a word that shall not return: 'To me every knee shall bow, every tongue shall swear.' Only in the Lord, it shall be said of me, are righteousness and strength; to him shall come and be ashamed, all who were incensed against him. In the Lord all the offspring of Israel shall triumph and glory" (Isa. 45:22-25).

Day 4

Praise the Lord! For it is good to sing praises to our God; for he is gracious, and a song of praise is seemly. The Lord builds up Jerusalem; he gathers the outcasts of Israel. He heals the brokenhearted, and binds up their wounds. He determines the number of the stars, he gives to all of them their names. Great is our Lord, and abundant in power; his understanding is beyond measure. The Lord lifts up the downtrodden, he casts the wicked to the ground. Sing to the Lord with thanksgiving; make melody to our God upon the lyre! He covers the heavens with clouds, he prepares rain for the earth, he makes grass grow upon the hills. He gives to the beasts their food, and to the young ravens which cry. His delight is not in the strength of the horse, nor his pleasure in the legs of a man; but the Lord takes pleasure in those who fear him, in those who hope in his steadfast love. Praise the Lord, O Jerusalem! Praise your God, O Zion! (Ps. 147:1-12).

Day 5

Bless the Lord, O my soul; and all that is within me, bless his holy name! Bless the Lord, O my soul, and forget not all his benefits, who forgives all your iniquity, who heals all your diseases, who redeems your life from the Pit, who crowns you with steadfast love and mercy, who satisfies you with good as long as you live so that your youth is renewed like the eagle's. The Lord works vindication and justice for all who are oppressed. He made known his ways to Moses, his acts to the people of Israel. The Lord is merciful and gracious, slow to anger and abounding in steadfast love. He will not always chide, nor will he keep his anger for ever. He does not deal with us according to our sins, nor requite us according to our iniquities. For as the heavens are high above the earth, so great is his steadfast love toward those who fear him; as far as the east is from the west, so far does he remove our transgressions from us. As a father pities his children, so the Lord pities those who fear him. For he knows our frame; he remembers that we are dust. As for man, his days are like grass; he flourishes like a flower of the field; for the wind passes over it, and it is gone, and its place knows it no more. But the steadfast love of the Lord is from everlasting to everlasting upon those who fear him, and his righteousness to children's children, to those who keep his covenant and remember to do his commandments. The Lord has established his throne in the heavens, and his kingdom rules over all. Bless the Lord, O you his angels, you mighty ones who do his word, hearkening to the voice of his word! Bless the Lord, all his hosts, his ministers that do his will! Bless the Lord, all his works, in all places of his dominion. Bless the Lord, O my soul! (Ps. 103).

Day 6

Make a joyful noise to the Lord, all the lands! Serve the Lord with gladness! Come into his presence with singing! Know that the Lord is God! It is he that made us, and we are his; we are his people, and the sheep of his pasture. Enter his gates with thanksgiving, and his courts with praise! Give thanks to him, bless his name! For the Lord is good; his steadfast love endures for ever, and his faithfulness to all generations (Ps. 100).

Day 7

Praise the Lord. I will give thanks to the Lord with my whole heart, in the company of the upright, in the congregation. Great are the works of the Lord, studied by all who have pleasure in them. Full of honor and majesty is his work, and his righteousness endures for ever. He has caused his wonderful works to be remembered; the Lord is gracious and merciful. He provides food for those who fear him; he is ever mindful of his covenant. He has shown his people the power of his works, in giving them the heritage of the nations. The works of his hands are faithful and just, all his precepts are trustworthy, they are established for ever and ever, to be performed with faithfulness and uprightness. He sent redemption to his people; he has commanded his covenant for ever. Holy and terrible is his name! The fear of the Lord is the beginning of wisdom; a good understanding have all those who practice it. His praise endures for ever! (Ps. 111)

III

How to Lead
a Prayer Workshop

14

Be a Qualified Leader

*T*o be a good leader you must be willing to spend from four to six weeks prior to the date set for the workshop sessions preparing yourself by actually immersing yourself in the study material and getting your own prayer diary started. This isn't something you can read over the night before or even a week before the first session. You have to live with the material and ideas and let them become part of your life. It takes an extended period of time to absorb the meaning—you must actually live it and use it.

This preparation is important in many ways. You must understand the purpose and material and not allow someone else to assume the leadership role. As the leader you must be willing and able to gently but firmly set limits on the group. Do not allow one or two people to dominate and control the conversation. You are responsible for the tone of the group. This is of utmost importance. As we stated in the introduction, the purpose of this study is to open the heart, mind and soul to God the Father. The only "test of fellowship," the only requirement, is that each participant believe in Jesus Christ as the son of God and as his personal Savior and Lord. No one should feel a "put down" or that they will be ashamed if they are open and honest about their feelings.

This is the key to the group—keeping it open and honest. In order to do this there must be an assurance of maintaining the integrity of the participants. What is said in the context of the group could be misunderstood if repeated outside. Individual statements or comments must never be used as dinner party conversation. You, as the leader, are responsible for seeing that this integrity is maintained.

As you get to know your members, you will become sensitive to the needs of the group as a whole and individually. Some may never say a word and communicate only through body language. Don't be disturbed. This may be all they are able to do at this time in their lives. Some people do not verbalize well and may be hurting so deeply that one word would bring on a cascade of tears. You will probably see a gradual change in these people, but it may not come till much later. As we said earlier, the *tone* of the group is important. It should be warm, loving, and caring.

15

Suggested Procedures for Twelve Study Sessions

*T*his study has been designed with church programs in mind. It is flexible and has been used successfully in these ways: (1) as a work/study program for any adult age Church School class; (2) Bible study groups; (3) as a Church Training study; (4) as a singles/career focus study and discussion group; (5) for a home study group; (6) the focus study of a retreat; and (7) as the pastor's prayer group with limited enrollment, keeping waiting lists when needed which creates interest as well as the incentive of "getting to know the pastor better."

The suggested outlines for the twelve sessions are very sketchy and should be used as an aid to your own teaching ideas. The sessions are best set up with the pattern of modern church school teaching methods; that is, a brief lecture or teaching time with ample time for directed discussions.

This twelve-week study can easily be modified to one-hour or ninety-minute sessions for six to eight weeks or for a two-to-three-day retreat.

The correlation of the study material, the meditations and the diary is important. For each petition there are seven days of meditations based on that particular theme. This gives a week to concentrate on each petition in turn. Each day during that week there is a meditation especially geared to help deepen the understanding of that petition. This pattern is followed throughout. So study, meditate and pray—they all fit together.

Session One

After you have welcomed the group and introduced the course, ask each person to write down in the back of their notebook what they want from this study. At the end of the course they can go back and see if this is what they received or if perhaps their goals changed in midstream.

Explain the use of the prayer diary and encourage the use of it. Challenge them to at least have gone through it once by the next session. Go through the suggested pattern for the prayer diary step by step with them now. This will help them get the feel of it and you can briefly give a few general ideas about each petition.

Teach the material in the Introduction. Trace the prayers of the Old Testament by having the group read in their Bibles the scripture listed in the Introduction. Discuss the material given in both the Preface and Introduction.

It is important for the group to feel that the tone of the group is warm and open.

Session Two

Preparation: Write the following topics on the chalkboard or have them on separate sheets of paper.

a. Discuss how to pray using these scriptures as guides: John 14:13, 14; Acts 4:12; Matthew 6:9-13; Matthew 18:19, 20.

b. What does the Bible teach about prayer promises? Mark 11:22-24; John 14:13-14; John 15:7 (give special attention to word *abide*); John 16:23-24.

c. Why can't I get through to God? Use material under that topic in the study guide.

d. Does prayer ever fail? Use material under that topic in study guide with these scriptures: Isaiah 1:15; Isaiah 59:1-3; Psalm 66:18; James 4:2, 3; Matthew 5:8; Matthew 27:46.

   What do you know about grace and despair? Use material in study guide. Are there any examples in the Bible? Personal examples?

Divide the students into five groups. Assign each group one of the topics and allow seven to ten minutes for them to discuss and come up with a presentation to the whole group. Each group should appoint their spokesperson but allow free discussion after the initial report has been given. As the leader be sure you maintain control and guide the discussion. According to your schedule you may limit the discussion of each topic. Closing: lead in a directed prayer time.

Session Three

Have these scriptures ready to hand out for students to read: Mark 14:36; Romans 8:15; Galatians 4:6; John 17:20-23; Matthew 6:5-14; Matthew 6:25-33; Matthew 10:29-31; Matthew 7:7-11; Romans 8:14-17; Exodus 33:17; Isaiah 45:3; Luke 15:11-32; Acts 4:12.

Ask for descriptive terms for Father and Mother. Make two lists on the chalkboard—the positive characteristics on one side and the negative ones on the other. Would you add any to broaden the description of the heavenly Father? Lead the discussion by asking questions like: "Would an orphan have a problem relating to God as Father? What about the children we hear about in child abuse cases? What about the drunken father, etc.? Now ask for the scripture to be read pertaining to the Father. Add a comment when you feel necessary. Save the scripture on the prodigal son for last (Luke 15:11-32). Read it from a modern translation and let this be your closing.

Session Four

Preparation: If possible bring some masks or at least bring pictures of the Thespian masks. Observe people you are with this week and see if you can tell what is really behind their masks. Write the topics listed for discussion on the chalk-board.

Ask: "Do you have a mask for each day of the week? Do you have one for church? A different one for the office? Another one for the party? Would you like to throw them all

away and reveal the true you? Divide the class into three
groups to discuss and bring back a report on these topics:
1. Honor—God's name or mine?
2. Hypocrites and my life—is there any connection?
3. Hallowed be Thy name—what has that to do with
   incarnation?
Use the study and meditation material on the second petition as resource material.

Session Five

Preparation: Select four or five people to take part in a
panel discussion concerning this third petition. Call them
early in the week and suggest that they study the material
thoroughly. You will be the moderator. Plan your questions
carefully and then give time for questions from the floor. You
are in charge and must guide the discussion.
Introduce the panel and explain the following procedure:
1. Ask each panel member to describe in twenty-five
   words or less the Kingdom of God. Ample scripture is
   found in the study guide.
2. How can one enter the Kingdom of God?
3. Can the results of the Kingdom be seen? What are they?
4. Is it easy to pray "Thy will be done in my life"?
5. If I pray this, can I be exempt from trouble?
6. How can I find God's will?
You and the panelists will find help on all these questions
in the study guide.

Session Six

Preparation: This will be a good session to review briefly
all of the previous petitions. Perhaps you will want to assign
this task to individuals or you may do it yourself.
Ask for the review of the past five sessions. Give ample
opportunity for discussion and questions.
Begin discussion of the fourth petition using the first
meditation on this petition as an opening. What are some of
the necessities of life? List them as the group volunteers. Don't

forget to bring out the idea that we don't have to be anxious. We have no time but the present.

Assignment for next time: Bring everything you know about forgiveness to the next session. Be prepared to tell about a time in your childhood or more recently when you were forgiven.

Session Seven

Lead into the petition on forgiveness by relating something that happened to you. A leader is most effective when able to expose himself emotionally. By doing so, he encourages others to share more openly. In a setting of warmth and love, oneness and sharing can be most helpful. If there is hesitation, give the illustrations of Jesus found in the study material (Matt. 6:14-15). Let the discussion flow by itself with your guidance. You may want to use the scriptures and ideas found in the study material to amplify and underscore certain ideas. This petition of forgiveness is crucial to the Christian life. Be sure they get the message!

Session Eight

Preparation: Write the following topics on the chalkboard.
1. What exactly is meant by the term *tempted* or *tested?*
2. Is there evidence that Jesus experienced temptation?
3. In what way does the Bible talk about "the Evil One"? How can we recognize this "Evil One"?
4. What is the role of the church in relation to this petition?

Study these topics yourself and become comfortable with them. Make four groups. Assign one of the topics to each group and give them the appropriate amount of time to come up with a report for the whole group.

Session Nine

Preparation: Be sure there are hymnbooks available. Make a list of the praise hymns you will use and the page numbers.

Ask the group members to use sheets of paper out of the back of their workbooks. This will be for their own personal use. At the top of the page write: "I praise the Father for. . . ." Now ask them to make a list. No one will see it. (Allow approximately five minutes.)

Divide the students into groups of about four or five. Assign three or four praise hymns to each group and have each group prepare a report on the basic message of each hymn. Some suggested hymns are:

> I Will Sing the Wondrous Story
> Blessed Be the Name
> Praise Him! Praise Him!
> There Is a Name I Love to Hear
> Holy, Holy, Holy
> Praise to the Lord, the Almighty
> All People That On Earth Do Dwell

These reports should point up the fact that the writers of these hymns experienced heartache, fear, and all the other feelings that we have, but out of it all produced these magnificent statements of their faith. They were able to view their sorrows and trials in the light of the marvelous love of the Father, and above all, to praise his name.

If time allows, you may want to discuss the components of the church worship service. In every group there is a wide background of church experience. Many have always called the place of worship an auditorium rather than a sanctuary. Perhaps you may want to discuss the difference in the two concepts. (*Auditorium* goes hand in hand with "religious pep rally" while *sanctuary* denotes worship and a place of refuge. There are many references for this. Here are just a few: Psalm 96:6; Psalm 150:1; Isaiah 60:13; Ephesians 2:19-22.) As your closing prayer you may want to use Psalm 103 or your own original psalm of praise!

Session Ten

You will find help for this discussion under "Questions Most Asked About Prayer." Two good resource books are: *Survival Kit for the Stranded* by William L. and Carolyn Self and *No Pat Answers* by Eugenia Price.

Preparation: This session will require quite a bit of preparation on your part, but I think that you will find it worthwhile. This session can be a great source of strength for many who are "bleeding." Prepare two or three brief sketches showing ways that people respond to tragedy. Select participants who have a good imagination and who are not bashful. Write out the basic sketch and the idea you want portrayed and let them use their own words. This will be the basis for your discussion. Here are some ideas for the sketches.

1. A hospital room where the doctor, minister, patient and several family members are gathered to receive the heartbreaking diagnosis of incurable cancer. A well-meaning "religious" aunt comes in, hears the news, and immediately begins to spout phrases such as: "It is God's will. Don't cry, just remember that this is God's work. Be brave and praise the Lord."

2. The living room of a home where the mother and father of a rebellious teenage daughter face the fact that she has left home for parts unknown. In comes the well-meaning neighbor who has perfect children. She intimates that if they had done certain things differently (been more strict, more lenient, spent more time, changed schools, etc.) this wouldn't have happened. This is God's will because of the parents' past.

3. The cemetery where a child, the victim of a driver under the influence of alcohol, is being buried. People offer comforting words to the parents like: "Be thankful you had him to enjoy this long. He is better off because he won't have to endure life's hardships. This is God's will; so be brave and don't grieve."

4. The family room of a typical home. Mother and father are reading the paper. The phone rings and the

message is obviously distressing. The teenage daughter and her boyfriend have been apprehended shoplifting and both also charged with possession of drugs. The reaction: "We have tried to be good parents. Where did we go wrong? She is active in the church youth group and choir. The leaders must be doing something wrong. They are supposed to keep kids out of trouble."
Perhaps you will have your own sketches to use in place of these and you may not have time to use but one or two.

Explain that this session is designed to provoke individual soul-searching, and no plan will be given for solving the problems. It is hoped that the sketches and discussion will give new and deeper insight to the human predicament.

Session Eleven

Write the scripture references on the chalkboard that are listed in the study section "What Happens to People Who Pray?" Assign the scripture references to the members after you have divided them into appropriate groups. Instruct them to read the scripture and be prepared to give a brief description of what was taking place and what happened to the one praying. These scriptures show that many times unusual things happen to people who pray—they sometimes end up in strange and awful places (lions' den, the cross, etc.). Are you willing to take this risk?

Lead the discussion into the idea of exploring a few of the differences in prayer and in other forms of meditation (transcendental, for instance).

Closing: Remind the group that when we pray for God's will in our lives, it will not bring instant, miraculous happiness and the solution to all problems. Jesus was not released from his ordeal, but was given the power to go through it. We are praying for strength to face whatever situation we are in, conquer it and defeat it. This accomplishment brings true joy. Joy is the result of obedience to God, being in his presence. Pray for this joy.

Session Twelve

This will be a time of review. Encourage participation from the group members. Challenge the group to continue using the prayer diary and to continue to grow spiritually in a responsible way. Talk about the difference in *having* faith and in living *in* and *by* faith. The Holy Spirit lives within— Thy kingdom come! Call for volunteers to recap each of the petitions. Call for any questions or discussion on any of the topics which have been studied during the past few weeks. Ask for sentence prayers with you as leader closing.

IV

Your Own Prayer Diary

16

How to Set Up
Your Own Prayer Diary

*T*hese last pages are for you to cut out and place in your 5 x 7 loose-leaf notebook. After each petition place notebook paper as you need space to add your own prayer ideas. These added pages will always be changing so don't hesitate to cross out, check off, and add more pages.

For your private study you will need your Bible, a pen or pencil, a notebook (as previously described), and this book for study and meditation. Make notes as you go through each petition. You will find that this keeps you "on track" and your mind from wandering. As you become accustomed to the discipline, your mind will be opened to new ideas and God will have a chance to speak to you and deal with you in new ways. This is an exciting new adventure. Enter this study with an open mind and heart and you'll be ready to receive God's blessings.

You will go through *each petition every day.* If you do not have time to finish, you can start at that point next time. Sometimes if you are away from home, you can easily take your notebook with you and do this while waiting in a doctor's office, on an airplane, etc. Prayer is an attitude of life—not necessarily closed eyes and bent knees. In fact, this whole study will probably be done with your eyes open. It will seem like hard work at first, and you may feel tired yet excited. You will want to make note of your feelings. As you can see, this actually becomes *your* personal prayer diary.

Treat it as such. You will not want anyone else to read it if you use it properly and really write down your true thoughts and feelings. A husband and wife should not share a notebook. This is private and personal between each individual and God.

Be sure to date your requests. It will be interesting to go back a month or so later and see that the situation may have changed or you may realize that it isn't important anymore. Make a note concerning this change.

Leave room after each petition to add your ideas, names of people and things for which you want to pray. As you read scriptures and have time to think and meditate, you should make notes. Under each step we will make some comments that will help you get your thoughts in order. Then begin to list your concerns. We will list several examples to start your thoughts. We also have a separate section for special prayer requests, thanksgiving and praise, and victories.

My Personal Commitment

It should be understood that this is a practical, disciplined, personal program that should help the individual develop lifetime skills in prayer. The goal of this study is to help the individual develop a wholesome, responsible, disciplined prayer life that is theologically sound, non-pharisaical in tone, and that is supportive of the local church. This attitude is of supreme importance. It is not necessary to seek superficial spiritual goals, religious ecstasy, or mystical encounters. As you appropriate the great privilege of prayer as offered by Jesus, God will work in his own way his purposes in your life. The steps to a mature relationship to our Father are found in Matthew 6:5-14.

You will want to make a covenant with God to consistently set aside prayer and study time each day. If your schedule is uncertain, you will want to adjust your time when necessary. However, it is a real help to commit yourself to a particular time for study when possible. Here is a covenant for you to sign.

> I covenant with God and our group (if you are doing this study with a prayer class) to develop a systematic, disciplined prayer life along the lines discussed in this study. I will be at every session except in case of extreme emergency.

Signed _____

Date _____

My times for prayer are:

Sunday _____	Thursday _____
Monday _____	Friday _____
Tuesday _____	Saturday _____
Wednesday _____	

Our Father, which art in heaven (Matt. 6:9).

When we pray "Our Father," two things are settled. (1) The concept of a father provides the best understanding of the nature of God. Think of the finest father you can imagine—he is strong, provides for and protects his children. Think of the finest mother you can imagine—she has all the fine qualities of love, patience, understanding, and sacrifice for her children. Now in your mind put these finest, highest qualities of mother and father together under God our Father. Think of God as *your* Father. God the Father loves us with a love that will never let us go. God knows us by name. (2) This settles our relationship to our fellowman—*every* man is our brother. Look around at your family!

Thinking of these things, my prayer goals are:
1. To develop an intimacy and openness to God as Father.
2. To realize that as his child I have the responsibility to be a good family participant. To expect the benefits of the family I must be a responsible member.
3. Develop attitudes that will not grieve my Father.
4. Let me be bold to claim my heritage as stated in Romans 8:14-17.
5. Remembering that our family includes all races everywhere in the world I especially pray for: (name world leaders, missionaries, individuals whom you know worldwide).
6. Now continue with your own petitions as you meditate on Our Father.

Hallowed be thy name (Matt. 6:9).

"Hallowed be thy name" is the inescapable obligation of reverence in every area of our lives. This becomes a petition or prayer of repentance, of confession of sin. Hallowed be thy name" means that we are praying to the glory of God—not glory to ourselves. God's name is to be treated differently from all other names. Give God's name a position which is absolutely unique. We must seek to make God's name known throughout the world by words and actions.

As I think of these things, my prayer goals are:
1. To develop my capacity for reverence.
2. To bear a more wholesome witness to his name. I want people to know that I know him by the tone of my lifestyle.
3. Someone is always observing my attitudes, actions and expressions. I may influence for good or bad. Let it be good!
4. Let me not blaspheme God's name with my ideas, prejudices and attitudes that are not in keeping with his holiness, justice and love.
5. Let God's name be holy, not mine.
6. Now continue with your petitions as you meditate on "Hallowed be thy name."

Thy kingdom come. Thy will be done in earth as it is in heaven (Matt. 6:10).

The Kingdom of God is the reign of God in individual lives. It is *my* personal obedience to the will of God. This is a petition for personal growth. His will must grow in me until it is as natural to pray "Thy will be done" as it is to breathe. The Kingdom and God's will is a daily growing process. It is never completed. This is a petition for the church. We are to pray for the family of the Father (the church). We cannot separate social, political, professional or religious life from the Kingdom of God and the will of God. This is a petition for social justice, governments, etc.

As I think of these things, my prayer goals are:
1. Pray for the political and religious leaders of the world, our nation, state, and city.
2. Pray for our missionaries as a whole and by name. Make a list.
3. Pray for your church and her leaders. Make a list.
4. Pray for all churches who hold our Father in common.
5. Pray for strength and guidance and courage to walk through the hard places and come out stronger in your faith and better able to minister to others.
6. Now continue with your petitions as you meditate on "Thy kingdom come. Thy will be done."

Give us this day our daily bread (Matt. 6:11).

This is a simple petition for everyday needs. God cares for our bodies as well as our spirits and souls. We must live one day at a time and not be fearful and anxious about the future. We cannot be selfish in this prayer. Pray and work and be generous.

As I think of these things, my prayer goals are:

1. Daily necessities (list some which concern you; these may change from day to day or week to week).
2. Teach me to be unselfish. Let me not limit my generosity to my friends or those whom I know personally.
3. Help me learn to control my fears and anxieties.
4. Now continue with your petitions as you meditate on "Give us this day our daily bread."

And forgive us our debts, as we also forgive our debtors (Matt. 6:12).

Though I may be a good, decent person I fall short of what I *can* do and what I *should* be. The grudges I nurse, the wounds I whimper about, the ways I harm my body, my failure to visibly uphold right action, my failure to let my displeasure of wrong doing (such as by public officials) be heard in the proper ways—these are only a few of my sins. God the Father intends for our burden of guilt to be lifted. This forgiveness comes in direct proportion to our ability to forgive those who have become indebted to us.

As I think about these things and remember the words of Jesus in Luke 23:34, "Father, forgive them for they know not what they do," my prayer goals are:

1. I confess these sins (write them down; revise when needed).
2. I ask forgiveness, for all sins—known or unknown—so that I may be fit to pray for others.
3. I am hurt and angry with these people (list them); or, these people have offended me (list them).
4. Now pray for these people and forgive them yourself.
5. Lift my burden of guilt and help me learn to forgive.
6. Continue with your petitions.

And lead us not into temptation but deliver us from evil (Matt. 6:13, RSV).

Also read Matthew 4:1-11 as you begin this section. As long as we live and breathe on this earth we will be surrounded by temptation (testing) and the evil one setting snares to trap us. "I do not pray, O Father, that thou shouldest take them out of the world, but that thou shouldest keep them from the evil" (John 17:15). We shall never be free from the dangers of life. Life is but one long peril and temptation. Jesus directs us to pray to the Father for strength to ward off the devil's attacks. So long as we are within our Father's field of power *nobody* and *nothing* can break his power. He will be *with* us in temptation—he walks beside us and never lets us down. He does not spare us suffering, but he is on our side *with* us. We still have to bear the burdens of life, and he gets under the load with us. "For we have not a high priest who is unable to sympathize with our weaknesses, but one who in every respect has been tempted as we are, yet without sin. Let us then with confidence draw near to the throne of grace, that we may receive mercy and find grace to help in time of need" (Heb. 4:15, 16, RSV).

We must be realistic about the demonic powers of Satan. The petition literally translated reads: "deliver us from *the evil.*" Demonic power is so very dangerous because it cannot be recognized; he is a master of disguise. Satan makes evil seem interesting, enjoyable, sometimes idealistic and good. Do not be seduced and persuaded. Read over and over the temptation of Jesus, realizing that he rose from the visions of shimmering, dazzling kingdoms and bread for the world to walk the road of poverty and the valley of the shadow to the ultimate shame. Victory over Satan comes *after* the valleys and heartaches, the troubles and pain, because Jesus walked through the ultimate separation to resurrection. These trials and testings are temporary. We will be stronger and better able to love and minister to others as we are sifted and made fit for God's use (Luke 22:31, 32).

Thinking of these things, my prayer goals are:
1. Evil habits I wish to pray about: (list them)
2. Evil attitudes I wish to take to the Father: (list them)
3. Evil forces I wish to repel: (list)
4. Spiritual strengths I wish to develop: (list)

For thine is the kingdom, and the power, and the glory, forever. Amen (Matt. 6:13).

We trust God's power to answer our prayers and take care of the longings of our hearts. We pledge to live *reverently* knowing that the earth is permeated with divine glory. Can you truly be yielded to our Father? Pray for this. All power and glory is for God. Let this be your praise and thanksgiving section.

Amen—so be it!

Add a page here for your "Bless" list.